T0014092

The "I LOVE MY INSTANT POT®" Three-Step Recipe Book

From *Pancake Bites* to *Ravioli Lasagna*,
175 Easy Recipes Made in Three Quick Steps

Robin Fields

Adams Media
New York London Toronto Sydney New Delhi

Adams Media
An Imprint of Simon & Schuster, Inc.
100 Technology Center Drive
Stoughton, Massachusetts 02072

First Adams Media trade paperback edition September 2022

ADAMS MEDIA and colophon are trademarks of Simon & Schuster.

For information about special discounts for bulk purchases, please contact Simon & Schuster Special Sales at 1-866-506-1949 or business@simonandschuster.com.

The Simon & Schuster Speakers Bureau can bring authors to your live event. For more information or to book an event contact the Simon & Schuster Speakers Bureau at 1-866-248-3049 or visit our website at www.simonspeakers.com.

Photographs by James Stefiuk

Manufactured in the United States of America

1 2022

Library of Congress Cataloging-in-Publication Data
Names: Fields, Robin, author.
Title: The "I love my Instant Pot®" three-step recipe book / Robin Fields.
Description: First Adams Media trade paperback edition. | Stoughton, Massachusetts: Adams Media, 2022 | Series: "I love my" series | Includes index.
Identifiers: LCCN 2022014642 | ISBN 9781507219829 (pb) | ISBN 9781507219836 (ebook)
Subjects: LCSH: Smart cookers. | Pressure cooking. | LCGFT: Cookbooks.
Classification: LCC TX840.S63 F54 2022 | DDC 641.5/87--dc23/eng/20220429
LC record available at https://lccn.loc.gov/2022014642

ISBN 978-1-5072-1982-9
ISBN 978-1-5072-1983-6 (ebook)

Contents

Introduction **4**

1. Cooking with an Instant Pot® **5**

2. Breakfast **11**

3. Soups, Stews, and Chilis **29**

4. Rice, Beans, and Pasta **51**

5. Appetizers and Snacks **71**

6. Side Dishes **91**

7. Chicken Main Dishes **109**

8. Beef and Pork Main Dishes **133**

9. Fish and Seafood Main Dishes **155**

10. Vegetarian Main Dishes **173**

11. Desserts **193**

US/Metric Conversion Chart **217**

Index **218**

Introduction

With the Instant Pot®, if you can twist a lid and press a button, you can have a delicious meal ready in a fraction of the time you're used to. With minimal cleanup, fast prep time, and the power of a pressure cooker, the Instant Pot® is the perfect appliance for anyone, whether you're a beginner solo cook in an apartment, taking care of a busy family, or simply looking for the convenience of one-pot cooking.

The *"I Love My Instant Pot®" Three-Step Recipe Book* features recipes ranging from French Toast Casserole and Creamy Alfredo Penne to Honey Garlic–Glazed Salmon and Fudge Brownies, so odds are you'll find the Instant Pot® version of your favorite meal. And with each of the 175 recipes requiring just three steps, you'll find mealtime has been simplified even more. These recipes will help keep you out of the kitchen and busy doing the things you love.

Along with delicious recipes and mouthwatering photos, you'll also find a chapter on why the Instant Pot® will become your new favorite appliance, how to use every function on your Instant Pot®, the best accessories to use with it, and tips on safe removal. Once you have this background, cooking with the Instant Pot® will be as simple as 1, 2, 3—even for beginners.

If you're ready to reduce your time spent in the kitchen without sacrificing an ounce of flavor, keep reading. It's time to get cooking!

1

Cooking with an Instant Pot®

Learning to use a pressure cooker can feel intimidating at first, but trust me, you'll get the hang of it in no time. In fact, you'll soon wonder how you ever lived without it. This chapter will introduce you to all the Instant Pot® buttons, explain how and when to release pressure from the Instant Pot®, teach you how to keep the Instant Pot® clean, tell you about some accessories that can take your pressure cooking to the next level, and give helpful tips for making cooking as quick as possible. All recipes in this book were developed using the 6-quart Instant Pot® Duo Nova model. If you're using an 8-quart Instant Pot®, be sure to add at least ½ cup of additional liquid to the inner pot before cooking.

While this chapter will cover the basics of using your Instant Pot®, the first step is reading the manual that came with your Instant Pot®. Learning how to use the Instant Pot® thoroughly is the key to success and will familiarize you with trouble-shooting issues as well as safety functions. Reading over the manual for your specific model and doing the water test run will help you feel more confident. Confidence in

the kitchen is what ultimately leads to success in creating delicious meals.

Why Pressure Cooking?

Pressure cooking has always been popular, but with today's electric pressure cookers like the Instant Pot®, it's easier than ever to do. Here are some reasons why the Instant Pot® will become your favorite appliance:

- **It's fast and convenient:** You can spend less time in the kitchen cooking, without sacrificing flavor. This is especially helpful if you like to prepare your meals ahead of time in large batches.
- **It's smart:** Ever put dinner in the oven, then run off to do something else around the house and forget to go back when it's done? The Instant Pot® has you covered. It will automatically switch into Keep Warm mode once the timer goes off. No more burnt meals!
- **It uses less energy:** Most people use their oven to cook, but it definitely comes with a price. Besides heating up the house during hot weather, it can take hours to slow roast large cuts of meat,

and that takes its toll on your home's energy consumption. The Instant Pot® can perform the same functions as a stove and a slow cooker in less time, meaning less energy output.

- **There's less cleanup:** Who wants to clean half a dozen pans after a meal? The Instant Pot® one-pot technique means minimal cleanup, leaving you more time to do other things.

Now it's time to take a closer look at all the ways the Instant Pot® can prepare food.

The Functions of an Instant Pot®

As soon as you see the buttons on the Instant Pot®, you'll see the amazing range of tasks this tool can handle—it can steam vegetables, cook a whole chicken, and even make a smooth, delicious New York–style cheesecake.

The key is knowing how the cooking programs work on the Instant Pot® and when to use them. Once you have a basic understanding of the functions, you'll be well on your way to creating your favorite Instant Pot® meal.

- **Pressure Cook:** This will likely be your most used button. It allows you to manually program the pressure level and cooking time. Some older models of the Instant Pot® have a "Manual" button instead. These both do the same thing; the label has just been updated in newer models. The Plus and Minus buttons adjust the cooking time, and the Pressure button toggles between High

Pressure and Low Pressure. (High Pressure is the default, and all recipes in this book use High Pressure.) This button makes it easy to get your Instant Pot® started without much thought, especially once you're more comfortable with determining cook times.

- **Steam:** This button allows you to steam meats and vegetables. Steaming is an excellent way to cook because it allows the food to retain nutrients and keep a fresh flavor. The Adjust button allows you to choose 0–15 minutes of cooking. The quick-release option will prevent your fresh vegetables from getting soggy. The Instant Pot® heats while it builds pressure, so for some vegetables, setting it to 1 minute is all they need to reach a perfect tender-crisp texture!

- **Slow Cook:** This button allows the Instant Pot® to function as a slow cooker. This non–pressure cooking method allows your Instant Pot® to cook while being temperature controlled, similar to a slow cooker. The Low, Medium, and High options correspond to a slow cooker's Low and High settings. You should never use the Pressure Cooking lid while using this cook mode. Instant Pot® makes tempered glass lids to be used during Slow Cook mode, or you can use any clear lid with a vent hole that fits.

- **Soup/Broth:** This Instant Pot® mode can be adjusted depending on your soup contents. It defaults to 30 minutes and brings the soup to a low simmer to avoid overcooking. You can even sauté your vegetables right in the pot before adding the rest of your ingredients and going into a pressure cooking program.

- **Meat/Stew:** This button allows you to cook savory roasts, fall-off-the-bone ribs, hearty stews, and more in less time than using the oven. The mode can be adjusted based on meat texture, and the timer can be adjusted to increase time based on the type and size of the meat.
- **Egg:** This button allows you to cook boiled eggs quickly and easily. The mode can be adjusted to reflect your preference with soft-, medium-, or hard-boiled eggs. Since you steam the eggs rather than boil them, they are less likely to overcook and more likely to have fluffy yolks. Not to mention, they take less than 10 minutes, and you don't have to watch them.
- **Sauté:** This button helps you save time and add flavor to your meal before you begin a pressure cooking program. It allows you to pan-sear, stir-fry, and simmer to reduce liquids. With this function, it is important that you do not use the lid.
- **Cake:** This button allows you to cook moist cakes and even perfect cheesecakes. The mode allows you to choose a light or dense cake. The More function allows you to make creamy New York–style cheesecake—it will never crack or dry out!
- **Yogurt:** On most newer models you'll find the ever-useful Yogurt button. This function allows you to do everything from making an incredibly easy cold-start yogurt to proofing dough for your bread recipes. For the yogurt recipe in this book, you'll need a transparent slow cooker lid. You can buy an Instant Pot® tempered glass lid or simply use one you

already own that fits your pot as long as it seals in the heat.
- **Keep Warm/Cancel:** When the Instant Pot® is programmed, this button ends the cooking program and places it into standby mode. The Keep Warm function is automatically enabled after a cooking program, but it can be turned off by pressing the Cancel button or another program button (if you have more cooking to do). You will know it worked because the Keep Warm indicator light will turn off.

Locking and Pressure Release Methods

Locking the lid of the Instant Pot® is very easy, but it's important to do it properly. The lid fits in place on the pot, and when rotated 30 degrees clockwise, makes a small sound to let you know the position has been changed.

As the Instant Pot® builds pressure, an indicator will pop up to let you know that it is fully pressurized and ready to start counting down the timer. Sometimes this is accompanied by a little hiss of steam, but it should be relatively quiet. The amount of time it takes for the pressure to be reached depends on the length of the cooking program.

There are two ways to release pressure from the Instant Pot®, and then you can remove the lid.

Natural Release

The Instant Pot® will naturally release pressure after a cooking program has completed. The time this will take varies based on how long the meal has been cooking. Once the pressure indicator drops, you may take off the lid. Never force the lid off if it will not turn, and never attempt to take it off during a cooking program. (Refer to the manual if needed.) Allowing a natural pressure release is great for recipes with meat because it allows the meat to remain tender and retain moisture. Some recipes may call for a timed natural release followed by a quick release, while others require a full natural release.

Quick Release

To do a quick release, once the cooking program has completed, carefully turn the valve from Sealing to Venting to allow the steam to release. Be sure to stand back from the Instant Pot® as you do this and keep your hands clear of the steam. A quick release is complete when the float valve is down, indicating all the pressure in the pot is gone. A quick release is ideal for steamed vegetables because it helps prevent overcooking. A quick release usually takes 1–2 minutes.

Opening the Lid

Once the pressure indicator has dropped (regardless of which method you use), you may remove the lid. Simply turn the lid counterclockwise until it makes a sound indicating it is fully in the open position and aligns with the Open arrow. If the lid will not turn, double-check that the pressure is fully released and the valve indicator has dropped down.

Pot-in-Pot Accessories

Every Instant Pot® comes with a trivet, a metal piece that is placed in the bottom of the pot and elevates food. Pot-in-pot accessories are those that fit inside the Instant Pot®, usually placed on the trivet, while water is added to the bottom of the pot. These accessories can broaden the number of recipes you can make in the Instant Pot® and open up a new world of exciting possibilities.

- **Steamer basket:** You can set vegetables on the trivet to cook, but nothing can beat the convenience of a great steamer basket. A steamer basket will make removing vegetables a breeze and also comes in handy when you want to cook a dozen eggs or steam chicken or fish out of liquid.
- **Springform pan:** A 7" springform pan fits perfectly into both the 6-quart and 8-quart Instant Pot®. This is a great choice for making cheesecake. If you have a smaller Instant Pot®, use a 4" springform pan.
- **Cake pan:** Six-inch round cake pans and 7-cup Bundt pans make the perfect-sized cake for 4–6 people without excessive leftovers.
- **Egg bite mold:** For everything from fluffy and flavorful egg bites to perfectly portioned brownies, an egg bite mold is a great accessory for your Instant Pot®. Most molds come with seven individual cups for filling. The Instant Pot® version has wells that hold ¼ cup of liquid. Other brands may vary slightly in size.

Accessory Removal

These options help to remove food and Instant Pot® accessories safely.

- **Tongs:** These will be helpful when lifting meat in and out of the Instant Pot®. Tongs are also helpful when removing steamer baskets.
- **Small kitchen towel:** Sometimes a simple kitchen towel can be the best tool. For tasks like wiping condensation away and taking out a foil-covered pan, towels are always great to have around.
- **Sling:** There are a number of silicone slings available for purchase that comfortably fit under pans to help you lift them out of the Instant Pot® after cooking. Alternatively, you can easily make your own by folding over a long piece of aluminum foil so that the sides come up and over the sides of your pan. This is a good method for removing cooking dishes that may spill or items such as cheesecakes that require gentle removal.

Cleaning the Instant Pot®

Before cleaning, ensure that your Instant Pot® is completely cool and unplugged.

- **Inner pot, trivet, and sealing rings:** All these parts are dishwasher safe, but use the top rack. You can also hand-wash in hot, soapy water.
- **Heating unit:** This is the larger pot that the inner pot fits into. It's unlikely that this area will accumulate much grime, but wiping the inside of this unit with a damp cloth will keep it clean. Do not submerge in water.

- **Lid:** The lid can be disassembled to be cleaned. The sealing ring can be removed and washed with soap and water. If it smells strongly, try placing the clean ring in the freezer or soaking in vinegar. You can also buy multiple rings for specific types of recipes, so the smells don't affect the food. The pressure-release handle can be popped out and washed to ensure there are no particles causing blockage. The anti-block shield (the small basket under the lid) should be removed and cleaned regularly with soap and water. It blocks food from entering the pressure-release valve.
- **The outside:** Wipe the outside as well as the inside lid of the Instant Pot® with a damp cloth. After it's all clean, be sure all components are put back in the correct position before beginning your next cooking adventure.

Making Cooking As Quick As Possible

The Instant Pot® already significantly reduces the amount of time you'll need to spend in your kitchen preparing meals, and with only three steps for each recipe in this book, the path to low-effort recipes has never been clearer. Still, there are simple steps you can take to make your cooking as quick and easy as possible.

Set Up Your Workstation Before Starting

Preparing your ingredients beforehand is one of the most important time-saving tips. This includes chopping your vegetables. Nothing is more frustrating than having to stop cooking to do more prep.

Recipes go much more smoothly when you read through the ingredients and instructions, gather your materials, and then start.

Use Precooked Meats

To save time on cooking meats, try a precooked option! If a recipe calls for 2 cups chicken, you can easily swap in a portion of a rotisserie chicken that you picked up at the grocery store and get the meal done even faster! There are also precooked frozen options for sliced and shredded chicken that can be used.

Use a Food Thermometer

An instant-read digital food thermometer is an essential kitchen tool that will help you know exactly when your meat is cooked safely and to your liking. Take out the guesswork, avoid overcooked meats, and save yourself time by investing in one of these handy tools. They're very affordable and available right at the grocery store.

Cook Bigger Batches

You can quickly cook large quantities of food all at once in your Instant Pot® and separate them into completely different meals for your week. For example, if you make a double batch of Quick and Easy Penne (see recipe in Chapter 4), you can add chicken and Alfredo sauce to one batch for one meal, and meatballs and marinara sauce to the other batch for a meal later in the week.

Clean As You Go

Cleaning up is the most dreaded part of the cooking process, but you can simplify it by cleaning your workstation, dishes, and tools as you go. Your Instant Pot® makes cleanup even easier, condensing all the ingredients, messy sauces included, into just one pot.

2

Breakfast

Mornings are busy, but breakfast is still the most important meal of the day. Thanks to the time-saving Instant Pot®, you'll have no trouble preparing tasty and nutritious breakfasts that you and your family will love. And with many of the recipes in this chapter, you can just set the ingredients and let the Instant Pot® do the work while you get ready for your day. With such recipes as French Toast Casserole and Sausage Gravy, this chapter is loaded with breakfast favorites that will start your day on the right note!

Apple Cinnamon Oatmeal 12

Grits 12

Blueberry Pecan Oatmeal 13

Steel-Cut Oats 13

Yogurt 14

Breakfast Potatoes 15

Vegetable Frittata 16

Pancake Bites 18

Bacon and Onion Quiche 19

Breakfast Burritos 21

Three-Cheese Breakfast Strata 22

Egg Bites 23

Breakfast Sausage Links 24

Sausage Gravy 25

Cinnamon Coffee Cake 26

Breakfast Casserole 27

French Toast Casserole 28

Apple Cinnamon Oatmeal

This creamy and delicious breakfast is ready in less than 10 minutes.

Hands-On Time: 5 minutes
Cook Time: 4 minutes

Serves 4

1 cup old-fashioned oats
1½ cups water
1 cup whole milk
1 tablespoon salted butter
3 tablespoons light brown sugar, packed
2 tablespoons granulated sugar
1 medium Honeycrisp apple, cored and diced
1 teaspoon ground cinnamon
¼ teaspoon apple pie spice
¼ teaspoon salt

1 Place all ingredients in an Instant Pot® and stir to combine. Place the lid on the Instant Pot® and click into place to close.

2 Press the Pressure Cook button and adjust the timer to 4 minutes. When the timer beeps, quick-release the pressure until float valve drops. Unlock lid.

3 Use a rubber spatula to stir ingredients together. Serve warm.

PER SERVING:

CALORIES: 246 | FAT: 6g | SODIUM: 197mg | CARBOHYDRATES: 42g | FIBER: 4g | SUGAR: 24g | PROTEIN: 6g

Grits

This porridge-like dish can be enjoyed both savory (with the addition of salt, cheese, and butter) and sweet (with the addition of sugar).

Hands-On Time: 5 minutes
Cook Time: 10 minutes

Serves 6

1 cup stone-ground grits
3¼ cups water
¾ teaspoon salt
2 tablespoons salted butter
½ cup whole milk

1 Place grits, water, and salt in an Instant Pot®. Stir to combine.

2 Place the lid on the Instant Pot® and click into place to close. Press the Pressure Cook button and adjust the timer to 10 minutes. When the timer beeps, let the pressure release naturally for 10 minutes, then quick-release any remaining pressure until float valve drops. Unlock lid.

3 Stir in butter and milk until mixture is creamy and well combined. Serve warm.

PER SERVING:

CALORIES: 142 | FAT: 5g | SODIUM: 329mg | CARBOHYDRATES: 22g | FIBER: 1g | SUGAR: 1g | PROTEIN: 3g

Blueberry Pecan Oatmeal

If you're making this as a batch for the whole week, store in a tightly sealed container in the refrigerator and top with blueberries just before serving.

Hands-On Time: 5 minutes
Cook Time: 4 minutes

Serves 4

1 cup old-fashioned oats
2 cups water
½ cup whole milk
1 tablespoon salted butter
¼ cup granulated sugar
2 tablespoons flaxseeds
½ cup chopped pecans
1 cup blueberries

1 Place oats, water, milk, butter, sugar, flax-seeds, and pecans in an Instant Pot® and stir to combine. Place the lid on the Instant Pot® and click into place to close.

2 Press the Pressure Cook button and adjust the timer to 4 minutes.

3 When the timer beeps, quick-release the pressure until float valve drops. Unlock lid. Stir in blueberries. Serve warm.

PER SERVING:

CALORIES: 300 | FAT: 16g | SODIUM: 37mg | CARBOHYDRATES: 36g | FIBER: 5g | SUGAR: 19g | PROTEIN: 6g

Steel-Cut Oats

Feel free to stir in your favorite toppings such as yogurt, jam, or brown sugar. Try topping it with something sweet followed by a crunchy element such as chopped nuts or toasted coconut.

Hands-On Time: 5 minutes
Cook Time: 10 minutes

Serves 4

1 cup steel-cut oats
3 cups water
¼ teaspoon salt

1 Place all ingredients in an Instant Pot® and stir to combine. Place the lid on the Instant Pot® and click into place to close.

2 Press the Pressure Cook button and adjust the timer to 10 minutes. When the timer beeps, allow a full natural release of pressure until float valve drops. Unlock lid.

3 Use a rubber spatula to stir oats. Serve warm.

PER SERVING:

CALORIES: 170 | FAT: 3g | SODIUM: 145mg | CARBOHYDRATES: 29g | FIBER: 5g | SUGAR: 0g | PROTEIN: 7g

Yogurt

Making your own yogurt couldn't be easier. Some recipes require a boil to begin, but this cold start simply adds all the ingredients and lets the Instant Pot® work its magic. For this recipe, be sure that your milk is ultra-pasteurized. Fairlife milk is a good option for this and can be found in the specialized dairy section of most grocery stores. For the yogurt starter, read the label closely to ensure that it does include active bacterial cultures.

Hands-On Time: 5 minutes
Cook Time: 8 hours

Serves 12

52 ounces ultra-pasteurized milk
2 tablespoons plain, full-fat Greek yogurt with active cultures

SWEETENER OPTIONS

This yogurt provides you with an unsweetened base. You can add your favorite sweetener such as granulated sugar, honey, stevia, or Splenda Zero Calorie Sweetener once the yogurt has chilled. You can also add 1 teaspoon vanilla extract after it has chilled for additional flavor.

1 Pour milk into an Instant Pot®. Whisk in yogurt until well combined, then place a glass slow cooker lid on the pot.

2 Press the Yogurt button and adjust the timer to 8 hours. The timer will count up from zero. Do not remove the lid during this time.

3 When the timer beeps, do not stir yogurt. It should look thick and creamy, not runny. A spoon will be able to stand by itself in the center of the pot. Place a paper towel between the lid and the bowl to absorb excess moisture, then place the pot in the refrigerator to chill at least 8 hours. Stir well and serve chilled or transfer to a covered bowl or container and store in the refrigerator for up to 2 weeks.

PER SERVING:

CALORIES: 83 | **FAT:** 4g | **SODIUM:** 65mg | **CARBOHYDRATES:** 3g | **FIBER:** 0g | **SUGAR:** 3g | **PROTEIN:** 7g

Breakfast Potatoes

This dish can be the perfect side or even the star of the plate. These potatoes are fluffy inside with a golden-brown exterior. Steaming the potatoes takes the guesswork out of frying because they're already fully cooked when they go into the oil. You won't want to leave out the seasoned salt on these; it's a quick way to add lots of flavor to this dish.

Hands-On Time: 5 minutes
Cook Time: 9 minutes

Serves 6

1 cup water
3 medium russet potatoes, cut into 1" cubes
2 tablespoons vegetable oil
1 medium green bell pepper, seeded and chopped
1 medium red bell pepper, seeded and chopped
½ medium yellow onion, peeled and chopped
2 tablespoons salted butter
1½ teaspoons seasoned salt
½ teaspoon ground black pepper
¼ teaspoon garlic powder
¼ teaspoon paprika

1 Pour water into an Instant Pot® and place a steamer basket in the pot. Place potatoes in basket. Place the lid on the Instant Pot® and click into place to close. Press the Pressure Cook button and adjust the timer to 2 minutes. When the timer beeps, quick-release the pressure until float valve drops. Unlock lid. Potatoes should be fork-tender but not overly soft. Place potatoes in a medium bowl of cold water to quickly stop additional cooking and set aside.

2 Press the Cancel button and pour out the water from the pot and wipe dry. Press the Sauté button on the Instant Pot® and allow to heat until the display reads "Hot." Add vegetable oil, bell peppers, and onion to the pot. Sauté 3 minutes until vegetables begin to soften.

3 Drain potatoes well and pat dry with paper towels. Return potatoes to the pot and add butter. Sprinkle with seasoned salt, black pepper, garlic powder, and paprika. Sauté potatoes until golden brown, about 4 minutes. Serve warm.

PER SERVING:

CALORIES: 173 | **FAT:** 8g | **SODIUM:** 423mg | **CARBOHYDRATES:** 22g | **FIBER:** 3g | **SUGAR:** 3g | **PROTEIN:** 3g

Vegetable Frittata

Treat yourself to the morning you deserve by getting your vegetables in first thing! This frittata is a warm, delicious, and nutritious meal to keep you full and focused for the day ahead. The feta adds a great tang to the dish and adds extra creaminess.

Hands-On Time: 10 minutes
Cook Time: 20 minutes

Serves 4

6 large eggs
½ cup half-and-half
1 medium red bell pepper, seeded and finely chopped
1 cup chopped broccoli florets
1 cup halved grape tomatoes
½ cup crumbled feta cheese
1 teaspoon salt
¼ teaspoon ground black pepper
1 cup water

1 In a large bowl, whisk together eggs and half-and-half. Mix in bell pepper, broccoli, grape tomatoes, feta, salt, and black pepper until well combined.

2 Spray a 6" round baking pan with nonstick cooking spray. Pour mixture into prepared pan and cover pan tightly with aluminum foil. Pour water into an Instant Pot® and place the trivet in the pot, then place pan on trivet.

3 Place the lid on the Instant Pot® and click into place to close. Press the Pressure Cook button and adjust the timer to 20 minutes. When the timer beeps, let the pressure release naturally for 10 minutes, then quick-release any remaining pressure until float valve drops. Unlock lid. When done, frittata will feel firm in the center and vegetables will be soft. Serve warm.

PER SERVING:

CALORIES: 219 | **FAT:** 14g | **SODIUM:** 882mg | **CARBOHYDRATES:** 7g | **FIBER:** 2g | **SUGAR:** 5g | **PROTEIN:** 14g

Pancake Bites

Whether you're looking for a creative spin on breakfast or enjoying them on the go, these Pancake Bites are the ultimate kid-friendly morning meal to get those bellies full and ready for the day. A silicone egg bite mold is the perfect accessory for cooking these pancakes just right. (For this recipe, you will need two molds, each with seven wells.) Don't forget the syrup!

Hands-On Time: 10 minutes
Cook Time: 12 minutes

Serves 7

½ cup all-purpose flour
½ teaspoon baking powder
¼ teaspoon baking soda
¼ teaspoon salt
¼ cup vegetable oil
½ cup granulated sugar
1 large egg
1 teaspoon vanilla extract
½ cup whole milk
1 cup water

CUSTOMIZE IT!

Try these with your favorite add-ins such as chocolate chips or chopped fruit. Simply place a few chocolate chips or ½ tablespoon chopped fresh fruit in each well before pouring in the batter.

1 In a large bowl, whisk together flour, baking powder, baking soda, and salt. Add oil, sugar, egg, vanilla, and milk and whisk until smooth.

2 Pour 3 tablespoons batter into each ungreased egg bite mold (fourteen wells total). Cover molds tightly with aluminum foil or a fitted silicone cover. Pour water into an Instant Pot® and place the trivet in the pot, then place filled molds on trivet, stacking as needed.

3 Place the lid on the Instant Pot® and click into place to close. Press the Pressure Cook button and adjust the timer to 12 minutes. When the timer beeps, quick-release the pressure until float valve drops. Unlock lid. Allow bites to cool at least 5 minutes before removing. Serve warm.

PER SERVING:

CALORIES: 184 | FAT: 9g | SODIUM: 180mg | CARBOHYDRATES: 22g | FIBER: 0g | SUGAR: 15g | PROTEIN: 2g

Bacon and Onion Quiche

Who doesn't enjoy a breakfast bursting with savory flavor? Each fluffy bite of this quiche has a delicious caramelized onion flavor. It's perfect for brunch and even meal prepping. You can enjoy this all week long with just about a half hour in the kitchen. Feel free to add 1 cup shredded Gruyère or smoked Cheddar if you like a cheesy quiche.

Hands-On Time: 10 minutes
Cook Time: 24 minutes 30 seconds

Serves 4

2 slices bacon, chopped
½ medium yellow onion, peeled and chopped
6 large eggs
½ cup whole milk
¼ teaspoon salt
1 cup water

1 Press the Sauté button on an Instant Pot® and allow to heat until the display reads "Hot." Place bacon in the pot and sauté until crispy, about 4 minutes. Add onion and sauté 30 seconds until softened, then transfer mixture to a large bowl. Press the Cancel button. Carefully remove the inner pot with potholders and let it cool for 5 minutes. Wash and dry the pot, then return it to the heating element.

2 Add eggs, milk, and salt to the bowl with bacon and onion and whisk until well combined. Spray a 6" round baking pan with nonstick cooking spray. Pour mixture into prepared pan and cover pan tightly with aluminum foil. Pour water into the Instant Pot® and place the trivet in the pot, then place the covered pan on the trivet.

3 Place the lid on the Instant Pot® and click into place to close. Press the Pressure Cook button and adjust the timer to 20 minutes. When the timer beeps, quick-release the pressure until float valve drops. Unlock lid. When done, quiche should feel firm in the center. Remove the pan and let it cool on the countertop 10 minutes before slicing quiche. Serve warm.

PER SERVING:

CALORIES: 189 | FAT: 13g | SODIUM: 357mg | CARBOHYDRATES: 3g | FIBER: 0g | SUGAR: 3g | PROTEIN: 12g

Breakfast Burritos

This recipe uses only the Sauté function to make a big batch of delicious filling. This is perfect for large get-togethers or making batches to freeze. Feel free to customize this recipe and add your favorite ingredients, such as salsa or sliced scallions.

Hands-On Time: 10 minutes
Cook Time: 15 minutes

Serves 12

- 2 pounds ground pork breakfast sausage
- 12 large eggs, whisked
- 1 cup shredded mild Cheddar cheese
- 1 teaspoon salt
- ½ teaspoon ground black pepper
- 12 (10") flour tortillas

---

1 Press the Sauté button on an Instant Pot® and allow to heat until the display reads "Hot." Break sausage into small pieces and place in the pot. Brown sausage until no pink remains, about 10 minutes. Drain excess fat.

2 Pour whisked eggs into the pot with sausage and mix to scramble eggs, about 5 minutes. Fold in Cheddar and sprinkle with salt and pepper.

3 Place ½ cup mixture on each tortilla and roll into a burrito. Serve warm or wrap in aluminum foil and refrigerate for up to 5 days. Burritos can be frozen as well. Place wrapped burritos in a resealable freezer bag and store for up to two months. To reheat, remove from foil and wrap in a damp paper towel. Place on a microwave-safe plate and microwave 90 seconds.

PER SERVING:

CALORIES: 485 | FAT: 21g | SODIUM: 887mg | CARBOHYDRATES: 38g | FIBER: 2g | SUGAR: 3g | PROTEIN: 28g

Three-Cheese Breakfast Strata

A strata is a savory bread pudding that can take your breakfast spread to the next level. It's also a great way to use your day-old crusty bread. This Three-Cheese Breakfast Strata is loaded with flavor.

Hands-On Time: 10 minutes
Cook Time: 30 minutes

Serves 6

3 cups day-old sourdough bread, cut into 1" cubes
4 tablespoons salted butter, melted
4 large eggs
½ cup whole milk
2 teaspoons Dijon mustard
1 teaspoon salt
¼ teaspoon ground black pepper
½ cup shredded sharp Cheddar cheese
½ cup shredded Gruyère cheese
¼ cup grated Parmesan cheese
1 cup water
2 tablespoons minced chives

BROIL

If you'd like to crisp up the bread pieces and brown the cheese for an extra crispness and visual effect, place the uncovered pan in the oven and broil 5 minutes until golden brown.

1 Spray a 6" springform pan with nonstick cooking spray. Place bread in prepared pan and gently press toward the bottom. Pour butter over bread.

2 In a large bowl, whisk eggs, milk, mustard, salt, pepper, Cheddar, Gruyère, and Parmesan, then pour mixture over bread, coating as evenly as possible. Cover pan tightly with aluminum foil.

3 Pour water into an Instant Pot® and place the trivet in the pot, then place prepared pan on trivet. Place the lid on the Instant Pot® and click into place to close. Press the Pressure Cook button and adjust the timer to 30 minutes. When the timer beeps, let the pressure release naturally for 10 minutes until float valve drops. Unlock lid. The center will be firm when strata is done. Garnish with chives. Serve warm.

PER SERVING:

CALORIES: 284 | FAT: 18g | SODIUM: 856mg | CARBOHYDRATES: 13g | FIBER: 1g | SUGAR: 3g | PROTEIN: 13g

Egg Bites

Once you see how easy these Egg Bites are to make, you'll make them over and over again. Besides the short cook time and amazing flavor, the best thing about these scrumptious bites is the endless ways you can customize them. Try switching up the meat and cheeses to find the flavor profile that best suits your morning.

Hands-On Time: 10 minutes
Cook Time: 10 minutes

Serves 7

4 large eggs
½ cup full-fat cottage cheese
½ cup shredded sharp Cheddar cheese
¼ teaspoon salt
7 tablespoons diced cooked ham
1 cup water

1 Place eggs in a blender, then add cottage cheese, Cheddar, and salt. Blend 20 seconds until smooth. Spray an egg bite mold with nonstick cooking spray, then pour egg mixture into mold, filling each well halfway. Add 1 tablespoon ham to each well and cover mold tightly with aluminum foil or a fitted silicone lid.

2 Pour water into an Instant Pot® and place the trivet in the pot, then place egg bite mold on trivet. Place the lid on the Instant Pot® and click into place to close.

3 Press the Pressure Cook button and adjust the timer to 10 minutes. When the timer beeps, quick-release the pressure until float valve drops. Unlock lid. Remove mold from the pot. Let egg bites cool 5 minutes, then remove from mold with a small rubber spatula. Serve warm.

PER SERVING:

CALORIES: 103 | FAT: 6g | SODIUM: 355mg | CARBOHYDRATES: 1g | FIBER: 0g | SUGAR: 1g | PROTEIN: 9g

Breakfast Sausage Links

Sausage links are a staple when it comes to breakfast. At first they can be tricky to cook because the outside might get too dark before the inside is fully cooked. The key is to cook them in water first and then sauté them. Steaming allows the links to stay juicy on the inside, then once they're fully cooked you can brown them as much as you'd like without concern of the middle being underdone.

Hands-On Time: 5 minutes
Cook Time: 8 minutes

Serves 6

12 ounces pork breakfast
   sausage links
1 cup water
1 tablespoon vegetable oil

1 Place sausage in the Instant Pot® and pour in water. Place the lid on the Instant Pot® and click into place to close. Press the Pressure Cook button and adjust the timer to 5 minutes. When the timer beeps, quick-release the pressure until float valve drops. Unlock lid. When done, sausage links should have an internal temperature of at least 145°F.

2 Use tongs to remove sausage links and set aside. Press the Cancel button. Pour liquid out of the pot, wipe dry, and return to the base. Press the Sauté button on the Instant Pot® and allow to heat until the display reads "Hot."

3 Spray the pot with nonstick cooking spray. Add vegetable oil, then add sausage. Cook sausage until golden brown, about 45 seconds per side. Serve warm.

PER SERVING:

CALORIES: 183 | **FAT**: 15g | **SODIUM**: 419mg | **CARBOHYDRATES**: 1g | **FIBER**: 0g | **SUGAR**: 1g | **PROTEIN**: 9g

Sausage Gravy

Gravy makes everything better, and there's no exception when it comes to breakfast. Cooking this on low will allow more fat to be rendered in cooking, making it even more delicious. This easy Sausage Gravy is the perfect companion for your eggs, biscuits, or just your spoon! If you're a fan of spice, try this recipe with a hot pork sausage.

Hands-On Time: 5 minutes
Cook Time: 21 minutes

Serves 4

- 1 pound ground pork sausage
- ¼ cup all-purpose flour
- 1 cup chicken broth
- ¾ teaspoon ground black pepper
- ¼ cup heavy whipping cream
- 1 cup whole milk

EXTRA-THICK GRAVY

For extra-thick gravy, whisk 1 tablespoon cornstarch in a small bowl with 2 tablespoons water until smooth. Stir this mixture in with the milk and it will further thicken up the gravy.

1 Press the Sauté button on an Instant Pot® and adjust the temperature to "Less," then allow to heat until the display reads "Hot." Add sausage to the pot. Cook and crumble sausage until no pink remains, about 10 minutes. Do not drain grease.

2 Press the Cancel button. Sprinkle flour in an even layer on top of sausage and grease. Allow flour to soak into grease, about 30 seconds. With a wooden spoon, gently stir mixture. Pour in broth, then add pepper. Use spoon to scrape away any browned bits from the bottom.

3 Place the lid on the Instant Pot® and click into place to close. Press the Pressure Cook button and adjust the timer to 6 minutes. When the timer beeps, quick-release the pressure until float valve drops. Unlock lid. Press the Cancel button, then press the Sauté button. Whisk in cream and milk and allow gravy to reduce and thicken 5 minutes. Serve warm.

PER SERVING:

CALORIES: 368 | FAT: 23g | SODIUM: 339mg | CARBOHYDRATES: 10g | FIBER: 0g | SUGAR: 4g | PROTEIN: 24g

Cinnamon Coffee Cake

This coffee cake is the ideal morning treat. It's lightly sweetened and goes perfectly with a morning coffee. The top and bottom of the cake have a delicious layer of pecans, brown sugar, and cinnamon, making each bite full of flavor.

Hands-On Time: 10 minutes
Cook Time: 40 minutes

Serves 8

1 cup chopped pecans
½ cup light brown sugar, packed
2 teaspoons ground cinnamon
1½ cups all-purpose flour
1 teaspoon baking powder
½ teaspoon baking soda
¼ cup salted butter, melted
1 cup granulated sugar
1 teaspoon vanilla extract
½ cup full-fat sour cream
2 large eggs
1 cup water

1   In a medium bowl, whisk together pecans, brown sugar, and cinnamon. In a large bowl, mix flour, baking powder, baking soda, butter, granulated sugar, and vanilla until well combined. Add sour cream and eggs and beat until a smooth batter is formed.

2   Spray a 7-cup Bundt pan with nonstick cooking spray. Place half of pecan mixture in prepared pan, then pour batter on top. Top with remaining pecan mixture. Cover pan tightly with aluminum foil.

3   Pour water into an Instant Pot® and place the trivet in the pot, then place Bundt pan on trivet. Place the lid on the Instant Pot® and click into place to close. Press the Pressure Cook button and adjust the timer to 40 minutes. When the timer beeps, let the pressure release naturally for 10 minutes, then quick-release any remaining pressure until float valve drops. Unlock lid. When done, cake should feel firm to the touch, and a toothpick inserted into the center should come out clean. Let cake cool 20 minutes, then invert onto a plate to serve.

PER SERVING:

CALORIES: 427 | FAT: 18g | SODIUM: 213mg | CARBOHYDRATES: 60g | FIBER: 2g | SUGAR: 213g | PROTEIN: 6g

Breakfast Casserole

This cheesy casserole is inspired by the flavors of a Denver omelet. The bell peppers add a bright pop of color to this easy meal. Each fluffy bite is loaded with savory vegetables. Feel free to customize it with your favorite vegetables and cheese, or any vegetables you need to use up. Chopped fresh spinach and chopped tomatoes are good substitutes.

Hands-On Time: 10 minutes
Cook Time: 25 minutes

Serves 4

6 large eggs
½ cup whole milk
1 teaspoon salt
¼ teaspoon ground black pepper
1 cup frozen shredded potatoes
1 cup diced cooked ham
1 medium green bell pepper, seeded and chopped
1 medium red bell pepper, seeded and chopped
½ medium yellow onion, peeled and chopped
1 cup water
1 cup shredded sharp Cheddar cheese

1 Spray a 6" round baking pan with nonstick cooking spray. In a large bowl, whisk eggs, milk, salt, and black pepper until well combined. Pour into prepared pan. Stir in potatoes, ham, bell peppers, and onion, then cover pan tightly with aluminum foil.

2 Pour water into an Instant Pot® and place the trivet in the pot, then place pan on trivet. Place the lid on the Instant Pot® and click into place to close. Press the Pressure Cook button and adjust the timer to 25 minutes. When the timer beeps, quick release the pressure. Unlock lid.

3 When done, casserole should feel firm in the center. Gently fluff casserole with a fork to mix all ingredients, then stir in Cheddar just before serving. Serve warm.

PER SERVING:

CALORIES: 361 | FAT: 19g | SODIUM: 1,381mg | CARBOHYDRATES: 16g | FIBER: 2g | SUGAR: 4g | PROTEIN: 27g

French Toast Casserole

If you love French toast, you'll enjoy this easy-prep recipe. It comes together quickly and lets you enjoy all the delicious cinnamon flavor in less time than cooking individual pieces of bread would. This recipe is perfect with day-old French bread, but feel free to use any other kind of bread you need to use up, such as Italian, challah, or brioche.

Hands-On Time: 10 minutes
Cook Time: 25 minutes

Serves 6

3 large eggs
½ cup whole milk
1 teaspoon ground cinnamon
1 teaspoon vanilla extract
¼ cup light brown sugar, packed
2 tablespoons granulated sugar
3 cups day-old French bread, cut into 1" cubes
1 cup water
2 tablespoons pure maple syrup
¼ cup confectioners' sugar

1 Spray a 6" springform pan with non-stick cooking spray. In a large bowl, whisk together eggs, milk, cinnamon, vanilla, brown sugar, and granulated sugar. Add bread cubes and toss until well coated.

2 Transfer bread mixture to prepared pan. Cover pan tightly with aluminum foil. Pour water into an Instant Pot® and place the trivet in the pot, then place pan on trivet. Place the lid on the Instant Pot® and click into place to close. Press the Pressure Cook button and adjust the timer to 25 minutes.

3 When the timer beeps, quick-release the pressure until float valve drops. Unlock lid. Remove pan from pot. Let rest 5 minutes before slicing into six pieces. Drizzle with maple syrup and sprinkle with confectioners' sugar to serve.

PER SERVING:

CALORIES: 182 | FAT: 3g | SODIUM: 152mg | CARBOHYDRATES: 32g | FIBER: 1g | SUGAR: 23g | PROTEIN: 6g

3

Soups, Stews, and Chilis

Soups, stews, and chilis are the ultimate comfort foods. Nothing beats a warm bowl of soup on a cold winter evening, whether you're feeling under the weather or simply craving something hearty. Many soup recipes require long cook times to create that bold and mouthwatering flavor that we all know and love. But by pressure cooking your soups, stews, and chilis, you can eliminate the need for all-day cooking and get your meal on the table in a fraction of the time. Even better, the Instant Pot® comes with a slow cooking function so you can make the cooking choice that works best for you and your schedule. From Red Chili to classic Chicken Noodle Soup, this chapter's recipes are full of a wide variety of flavorful ideas to keep your belly full of comfort and flavor!

Creamy Sausage and Tortellini Soup 30

Lasagna Soup 31

Tomato Soup 32

Wild Rice and Chicken Soup 33

Chicken Noodle Soup 35

Broccoli Cheddar Soup 36

Cheeseburger Soup 37

Beef Stew 38

Red Chili 39

Taco Soup 40

White Chicken Chili 42

Cabbage Roll Soup 43

Green Enchilada Chicken Soup 44

Steakhouse Potato Chowder 45

Tuscan Soup 47

Creamy Chipotle Chicken Soup 48

Tomato Lentil Soup 49

Creamy Sausage and Tortellini Soup

This soup is a creamy bowl of comfort food, filled with delicious sausage and vegetables. The tortellini add a nice cheese flavor. This soup pairs well with a fresh salad and a piece of crusty bread to scoop up all the flavorful leftover broth.

Hands-On Time: 10 minutes
Cook Time: 23 minutes

Serves 4

- 1 pound ground Italian sausage
- 1 medium yellow onion, peeled and diced
- 1 medium carrot, peeled and diced
- 1 stalk celery, trimmed and chopped
- 1 tablespoon tomato paste
- 1 (14.5-ounce) can diced tomatoes
- 32 ounces vegetable broth
- 1 teaspoon salt
- ¼ teaspoon ground black pepper
- 1 teaspoon Italian seasoning
- 19 ounces frozen three-cheese tortellini
- 2 tablespoons cornstarch
- ¼ cup heavy whipping cream

1 Press the Sauté button on an Instant Pot® and allow to heat until the display reads "Hot." Place sausage in the pot and sauté until no pink remains and it's broken into small crumbles, about 10 minutes. Drain grease and return the pot to the base. Add onion, carrot, celery, and tomato paste to the pot and sauté 3 minutes until vegetables begin to soften.

2 Press the Cancel button. Add diced tomatoes, broth, salt, pepper, Italian seasoning, and tortellini. Place the lid on the Instant Pot® and click into place to close. Press the Pressure Cook button and adjust the timer to 5 minutes. When the timer beeps, quick-release the pressure until float valve drops. Unlock lid and press the Cancel button.

3 In a small bowl, whisk cornstarch and cream until smooth. Press the Sauté button on the Instant Pot® and whisk in cornstarch mixture. Allow soup to thicken 5 minutes, stirring occasionally. Serve warm.

PER SERVING:

CALORIES: 716 | FAT: 34g | SODIUM: 3,134mg | CARBOHYDRATES: 68g | FIBER: 11g | SUGAR: 9g | PROTEIN: 33g

Lasagna Soup

This meal is packed with all your favorite lasagna flavors and none of the hassle. You can be enjoying a delicious bowl of soup in under 30 minutes from start to finish—less time than assembling and baking a whole lasagna. To save even more time, you can cook the beef and onion ahead of time so all you have to do for dinner is add all the ingredients to the pot and start cooking.

Hands-On Time: 20 minutes
Cook Time: 12 minutes

Serves 6

1 pound 70/30 ground beef
1 medium yellow onion, peeled and chopped
2 teaspoons Italian seasoning
1 teaspoon salt
¼ teaspoon ground black pepper
4 cups chicken broth
1 cup marinara sauce
2 tablespoons tomato paste
1 (14.5-ounce) can diced tomatoes, drained
8 lasagna noodles, broken into pieces
¼ cup full-fat ricotta cheese
½ cup grated Parmesan cheese

1 Press the Sauté button on an Instant Pot® and allow to heat until the display reads "Hot." Using a wooden spoon, break beef into pieces, then brown until no pink remains, about 7 minutes. Drain grease and return the pot to the base to continue sautéing. Add onion, Italian seasoning, salt, and pepper and stir to combine.

2 Press the Cancel button. Pour in broth, sauce, tomato paste, diced tomatoes, and broken noodles. Place the lid on the Instant Pot® and click into place to close. Press the Pressure Cook button and adjust the timer to 5 minutes. When the timer beeps, quick-release the pressure until float valve drops. Unlock lid. When done, noodles will be tender.

3 To serve, fill bowls with soup, then place small spoonfuls of ricotta on top. Finish with grated Parmesan.

PER SERVING:

CALORIES: 319 | FAT: 12g | SODIUM: 1,505mg | CARBOHYDRATES: 28g | FIBER: 3g | SUGAR: 7g | PROTEIN: 21g

Tomato Soup

Making your own tomato soup is easier than you think. The key is using San Marzano tomatoes. These plum tomatoes have a lower water content than other varieties, and they are sweet, which is what makes them so enjoyable for soups. This flavorful recipe pairs perfectly with a grilled cheese sandwich.

Hands-On Time: 10 minutes
Cook Time: 12 minutes

Serves 4

2 tablespoons salted butter
1 medium yellow onion, peeled and finely chopped
2 cloves garlic, peeled and finely minced
2 cups vegetable stock
1 (28-ounce) can crushed San Marzano tomatoes
2 large carrots, peeled and cut into thirds
1 teaspoon dried basil
½ teaspoon salt
¼ teaspoon ground black pepper
¼ cup heavy whipping cream

WHY CARROTS?

Tomatoes are naturally acidic. Many store-bought tomato sauces have added sugar in them, which often tempers acidity. Rather than add sugar to this recipe, carrots are cooked in the soup to impart flavor and natural sugar, which helps balance the acid level of the tomatoes. If you don't have carrots or cannot eat them, add 1 teaspoon granulated sugar to this recipe.

1 Press the Sauté button on an Instant Pot® and allow to heat until the display reads "Hot." Add butter and onion to the pot and sauté 2 minutes until fragrant. Press the Cancel button. Add garlic, stock, and tomatoes to the pot.

2 Add carrots to the pot. They will be removed later. Sprinkle in basil, salt, and pepper. Place the lid on the Instant Pot® and click into place to close. Press the Pressure Cook button and adjust the timer to 10 minutes. When the timer beeps, quick-release the pressure until float valve drops. Unlock lid.

3 Carefully remove carrots and discard. Press the Cancel button. Stir in cream. Use an immersion blender to blend soup until smooth, or transfer mixture to a blender and blend until smooth, about 3 minutes. Serve warm.

PER SERVING:

CALORIES: 183 | **FAT:** 11g | **SODIUM:** 985mg | **CARBOHYDRATES:** 18g | **FIBER:** 4g | **SUGAR:** 9g | **PROTEIN:** 4g

Wild Rice and Chicken Soup

This comforting soup is bursting with fresh vegetables. It is creamy and perfect for cold nights. The rice adds a delicious nutty flavor. This recipe calls for a wild rice blend rather than plain wild rice. The blend is more budget friendly than plain wild rice and tastes just as delicious. It's often a mix of wild rice, long-grain brown rice, sweet brown rice, and black rice.

Hands-On Time: 5 minutes
Cook Time: 35 minutes

Serves 8

- 3 cups shredded cooked boneless, skinless chicken breast
- 5 cups chicken broth
- 1 tablespoon salted butter
- 2 large carrots, peeled and finely diced
- 2 medium stalks celery, trimmed and diced
- ½ cup sliced cremini mushrooms
- 1 medium yellow onion, peeled and diced
- 1 cup wild rice blend, rinsed and drained
- 2 teaspoons Italian seasoning
- 1 teaspoon salt
- ¼ teaspoon ground black pepper
- ¼ teaspoon dried thyme
- ¼ teaspoon dried oregano
- ¼ cup heavy cream
- 3 tablespoons cornstarch

1 Place chicken, broth, butter, carrots, celery, mushrooms, onion, wild rice, Italian seasoning, salt, pepper, thyme, and oregano in an Instant Pot®.

2 Place the lid on the Instant Pot® and click into place to close. Press the Pressure Cook button and adjust the timer to 30 minutes. When the timer beeps, let the pressure release naturally for 5 minutes, then quick-release any remaining pressure until float valve drops. Unlock lid.

3 Press the Cancel button and then press the Sauté button on the Instant Pot®. In a small bowl, whisk cream and cornstarch together, then pour mixture into soup. Continue cooking on Sauté mode 5 minutes to allow soup to thicken. Serve warm.

PER SERVING:

CALORIES: 224 | FAT: 6g | SODIUM: 943mg | CARBOHYDRATES: 20g | FIBER: 2g | SUGAR: 3g | PROTEIN: 21g

Chicken Noodle Soup

It doesn't get much more comforting than Chicken Noodle Soup. This classic dish hits all the right notes with savory broth, vegetables, and perfectly cooked noodles packed into each warm bowl. This recipe uses precooked chicken to make it weeknight friendly. You can use canned chicken, a rotisserie chicken, or any leftover chicken you may have; just be sure to dice it into bite-sized pieces.

Hands-On Time: 10 minutes
Cook Time: 20 minutes

Serves 6

2 tablespoons salted butter

2 large carrots, peeled and diced

2 large stalks celery, trimmed and sliced into ¼" pieces

½ medium yellow onion, peeled and diced

32 ounces chicken broth

2 cups cubed cooked boneless, skinless chicken breasts

½ teaspoon salt

¼ teaspoon ground black pepper

¼ teaspoon garlic powder

¼ teaspoon dried thyme

2 cups uncooked egg noodles

1 Press the Sauté button on an Instant Pot® and allow to heat until the display reads "Hot." Place the butter, carrots, celery, and onion in the pot. Sauté 3 minutes until fragrant. Pour broth into the pot and scrape the bottom of the pot with a wooden spoon to remove any browned bits. Add chicken, salt, pepper, garlic powder, and thyme. Press the Cancel button.

2 Place the lid on the Instant Pot® and click into place to close. Press the Pressure Cook button and adjust the timer to 7 minutes. When the timer beeps, quick-release the pressure until float valve drops. Unlock lid. When done, vegetables should be tender.

3 Add noodles to the pot while keeping the Keep Warm mode on. Let noodles cook uncovered 10 minutes until tender, stirring occasionally. Serve warm.

PER SERVING:

CALORIES: 178 | FAT: 6g | SODIUM: 887mg | CARBOHYDRATES: 11g | FIBER: 1g | SUGAR: 2g | PROTEIN: 18g

Broccoli Cheddar Soup

This classic soup comes together in no time. It's creamy and light, making it the perfect choice for cold and hot days alike. The carrot adds not only a bright color but also sweetness to help neutralize any bitterness the broccoli may have. Each spoonful of this comfort meal is filled with soft vegetables and cheesy goodness.

Hands-On Time: 5 minutes
Cook Time: 5 minutes

Serves 4

- 2 tablespoons salted butter
- 1 tablespoon olive oil
- ½ medium yellow onion, peeled and diced
- 1 medium carrot, peeled and grated
- 2 cups chopped broccoli florets
- 3 cups chicken broth
- 1½ cups whole milk
- ½ teaspoon salt
- ½ teaspoon ground black pepper
- ¼ cup all-purpose flour
- 1 tablespoon cornstarch
- 1½ cups freshly shredded sharp Cheddar cheese

FRESHLY SHREDDED CHEESE
Be sure to use freshly shredded cheese for this recipe. Pre-shredded cheese is often coated in a thin layer of starch to help avoid clumps in dry packaging. For this recipe, the starch will heat and cause clumps of cheese to stick together. For a smooth cheesy soup, be sure to shred it straight from the block.

1. Press the Sauté button on an Instant Pot® and allow to heat until the display reads "Hot." Add butter, olive oil, onion, and carrot to the pot. Sauté 2 minutes until vegetables begin to soften.

2. Press the Cancel button. Add broccoli to the pot, then pour in broth. Place the lid on the Instant Pot® and click into place to close. Press the Pressure Cook button and adjust the timer to 3 minutes. When the timer beeps, quick-release the pressure until float valve drops. Unlock lid.

3. In a medium bowl, whisk together milk, salt, pepper, flour, and cornstarch. Whisk mixture into soup, then whisk in Cheddar. Continue whisking until all ingredients are smooth and soup thickens, about 4 minutes. Serve warm.

PER SERVING:

CALORIES: 382 | FAT: 24g | SODIUM: 1,366mg | CARBOHYDRATES: 20g | FIBER: 2g | SUGAR: 8g | PROTEIN: 17g

Cheeseburger Soup

This satisfying meal featuring tender beef and a smoky sauce is quick to make and bursting with flavor. Feel free to get creative and add your own twist with pickled jalapeños to make it spicy, or your favorite croutons for a crunch.

Hands-On Time: 10 minutes
Cook Time: 22 minutes

Serves 6

- 1½ pounds 70/30 ground beef
- 4 slices bacon, chopped
- 1 medium yellow onion, peeled and chopped
- 1 (14.5-ounce) can diced tomatoes, drained
- 1 teaspoon salt
- ¼ teaspoon ground black pepper
- 1 tablespoon Worcestershire sauce
- ½ teaspoon liquid smoke
- 1 tablespoon tomato paste
- 32 ounces vegetable broth
- 4 medium russet potatoes, peeled and cut into ½" cubes
- 2 tablespoons cornstarch
- 2 tablespoons water
- ¼ cup chopped dill pickles
- 1½ cups shredded sharp Cheddar cheese

HAMBURGER BUN CROUTONS

Turn slightly stale hamburger buns into easy croutons. Preheat the oven to 350°F and cut up 4 burger buns into 1" pieces. Drizzle with 2 tablespoons melted salted butter, then sprinkle with ¼ teaspoon each of salt, pepper, and Italian seasoning and place on a foil-lined sheet. Bake 8 minutes until golden.

1 Press the Sauté button on an Instant Pot® and allow to heat until the display reads "Hot." Add beef and bacon to the pot and sauté until beef is fully cooked and no pink remains, about 7 minutes. Drain grease and return the pot to the base. Add onion and diced tomatoes and sauté 2 minutes. Press the Cancel button.

2 Add salt, pepper, Worcestershire sauce, liquid smoke, tomato paste, broth, and potatoes to the pot. Place the lid on the Instant Pot® and click into place to close. Press the Pressure Cook button and adjust the timer to 8 minutes. When the timer beeps, quick-release the pressure until float valve drops. Unlock lid. When done, potatoes should be tender.

3 Press the Cancel button, then press the Sauté button. In a small bowl, whisk cornstarch and water until smooth, then pour mixture into the Instant Pot®. Allow 5 minutes for soup to thicken, stirring frequently. To serve, top with chopped pickles and Cheddar. Serve warm.

PER SERVING:

CALORIES: 470 | **FAT:** 21g | **SODIUM:** 1,492mg | **CARBOHYDRATES:** 33g | **FIBER:** 4g | **SUGAR:** 5g | **PROTEIN:** 29g

Beef Stew

One of the benefits of pressure cooking is that it imparts flavor and cooks quickly while not releasing moisture. It takes tough cuts of meat and makes them melt-in-your-mouth tender in less time and with less hassle than the stovetop or oven. This recipe is perfect for cold weather because it's packed with filling ingredients that leave you feeling warm and satisfied. This stew is best enjoyed with a piece of buttered bread or on top of mashed potatoes.

Hands-On Time: 10 minutes
Cook Time: 17 minutes 30 seconds

Serves 8

- 2 tablespoons olive oil
- 2 pounds beef stew meat, cut into 1" cubes
- 1 teaspoon salt
- ½ teaspoon ground black pepper
- 1 large yellow onion, peeled and chopped
- 2 large carrots, peeled and sliced
- 2 tablespoons Worcestershire sauce
- 2 cloves garlic, peeled and finely minced
- 2 medium russet potatoes, peeled and cut into ½" cubes
- 1 (8-ounce) can tomato sauce
- 2 tablespoons tomato paste
- 3 cups beef broth
- ¼ cup whole milk
- 1 tablespoon cornstarch

1 Press the Sauté button on an Instant Pot® and allow to heat until the display reads "Hot." Add olive oil and beef cubes, then sprinkle with salt and pepper. Sauté meat on each side until browned, about 45 seconds per side. Add onion, carrots, Worcestershire sauce, and garlic to the pot. Sauté 1 minute, then press the Cancel button.

2 Add potatoes, tomato sauce, tomato paste, and broth to the pot and stir to combine. Use a wooden spoon to scrape any browned bits from the bottom. Place the lid on the Instant Pot® and click into place to close. Press the Pressure Cook button and adjust the timer to 8 minutes. When the timer beeps, let the pressure release naturally for 10 minutes, then quick-release any remaining pressure until float valve drops. Unlock lid.

3 In a small bowl, whisk milk and cornstarch together. Whisk mixture into beef stew and allow stew to thicken, about 5 minutes, stirring occasionally while the pot remains on the Keep Warm setting. Serve warm.

PER SERVING:

CALORIES: 163 | FAT: 4g | SODIUM: 857mg | CARBOHYDRATES: 17g | FIBER: 2g | SUGAR: 4g | PROTEIN: 15g

Red Chili

There's nothing like a warm bowl of chili. On the stovetop it can take hours to allow the flavors to reach their full potential. With the Instant Pot®, the pressure forces the flavors to infuse more quickly and gets the meal finished in a fraction of the time. Top this delicious, chunky chili with your personal favorites such as shredded cheese, sour cream, or a dash of hot sauce.

Hands-On Time: 10 minutes
Cook Time: 40 minutes

Serves 8

- 2 pounds 80/20 ground beef
- 1 tablespoon salted butter
- 1 tablespoon olive oil
- 1 large green bell pepper, seeded and diced
- ½ medium white onion, peeled and diced
- 3 tablespoons chili powder
- 2 tablespoons ground cumin
- 1 teaspoon garlic powder
- 1 teaspoon salt
- ¼ teaspoon ground black pepper
- 2 tablespoons tomato paste
- 2 cups beef broth
- 1 (15-ounce) can diced tomatoes
- 2 (15-ounce) cans kidney beans, drained

1 Press the Sauté button on an Instant Pot® and allow to heat until the display reads "Hot." Place beef in the pot and break into pieces using a wooden spoon. Brown until no pink remains, about 7 minutes. Drain grease and return the pot to the base. While still in Sauté mode, add butter, olive oil, bell pepper, and onion. Sauté 2 minutes until fragrant.

2 Add chili powder, cumin, garlic powder, salt, black pepper, and tomato paste. Stir to combine, then sauté 1 minute. Pour in broth, diced tomatoes, and kidney beans, then stir to combine. Press the Cancel button. Place the lid on the Instant Pot® and click into place to close. Press the Pressure Cook button and adjust the timer to 20 minutes. When the timer beeps, let the pressure release naturally for 20 minutes, then quick-release any remaining pressure until float valve drops. Unlock lid.

3 To reduce chili to your desired thickness, press the Cancel button, then the Sauté button. It will warm, then begin to steam. Stirring frequently, allow chili to cook down 10 minutes, reducing the liquid and making chili thicker. Serve warm.

PER SERVING:

CALORIES: 362 | **FAT:** 16g | **SODIUM:** 956mg | **CARBOHYDRATES:** 22g | **FIBER:** 8g | **SUGAR:** 3g | **PROTEIN:** 28g

Taco Soup

This easy meal is perfect for weeknights. It's warm, comforting, and full of protein so you'll stay full. The ranch seasoning adds a zesty edge. This soup tastes even better with your favorite toppings such as shredded cheese, sour cream, sliced jalapeños, and crunchy tortilla strips, so add whatever you please.

Hands-On Time: 10 minutes
Cook Time: 15 minutes

Serves 5

32 ounces chicken broth
3 cups shredded cooked boneless, skinless chicken thighs
1 (15-ounce) can black beans, drained
1 (15-ounce) can chickpeas, drained
1 (7-ounce) can diced tomatoes and green chiles
½ cup chopped yellow onion
1 (1-ounce) packet taco seasoning
1 tablespoon dry ranch seasoning

1 Place all ingredients in an Instant Pot®. Stir until well combined. Place the lid on the Instant Pot® and click into place to close.

2 Press the Pressure Cook button and adjust the timer to 15 minutes.

3 When the timer beeps, let the pressure release naturally for 10 minutes, then quick-release any remaining pressure until float valve drops. Unlock lid. When done, broth should be red and beans and chickpeas should be soft. Stir soup, then serve warm.

PER SERVING:

CALORIES: 536 | FAT: 7g | SODIUM: 1,702mg | CARBOHYDRATES: 66g | FIBER: 16g | SUGAR: 11g | PROTEIN: 47g

White Chicken Chili

This creamy dish is a great alternative to beef chili. It has a subtle heat and goes perfectly with a scoop of sour cream and shredded cheese. If you're looking for more tang, try squeezing some fresh lime juice right on top before serving.

Hands-On Time: 10 minutes
Cook Time: 20 minutes

Serves 6

- 2 tablespoons olive oil
- 1 medium yellow onion, peeled and diced
- 1 (4.5-ounce) can green chiles
- 1 small jalapeño, seeded and chopped
- 2 medium green bell peppers, seeded and chopped
- 2 teaspoons ground cumin
- 1 teaspoon salt
- ½ teaspoon garlic powder
- ¼ teaspoon ground black pepper
- 2 cups shredded cooked boneless, skinless chicken breasts
- 2 (15-ounce) cans cannellini beans, drained and rinsed
- 32 ounces chicken broth
- 4 ounces cream cheese, softened
- 2 tablespoons cornstarch
- 3 tablespoons water
- ¼ cup chopped fresh cilantro

1 Press the Sauté button on an Instant Pot® and allow to heat until the display reads "Hot." Add olive oil, onion, green chiles, jalapeño, bell peppers, and cumin to the pot. Sauté 2 minutes until vegetables begin to soften. Press the Cancel button.

2 Sprinkle in salt, garlic powder, and black pepper. Add chicken, beans, and broth. Place the lid on the Instant Pot® and click into place to close. Press the Pressure Cook button and adjust the timer to 8 minutes. When the timer beeps, let the pressure release naturally for 5 minutes, then quick-release any remaining pressure until float valve drops. Unlock lid.

3 Press the Cancel button, then press the Sauté button. Stir in cream cheese until mixture is smooth. In a small bowl, whisk together cornstarch and water until smooth, then stir into chili. Let chili reduce and thicken 10 minutes, stirring frequently. Serve warm garnished with cilantro.

PER SERVING:

CALORIES: 330 | FAT: 12g | SODIUM: 2,229mg | CARBOHYDRATES: 31g | FIBER: 11g | SUGAR: 4g | PROTEIN: 25g

Cabbage Roll Soup

Cabbage rolls are delicious, but their preparation can be time-consuming. This soup makes things easy and brings you all the flavor with much less prep.

Hands-On Time: 10 minutes
Cook Time: 12 minutes

Serves 6

1 pound 70/30 ground beef
1 teaspoon salt
½ teaspoon dried thyme
½ teaspoon garlic powder
¼ teaspoon ground black pepper
1 medium yellow onion, peeled and diced
½ medium head green cabbage, cored and sliced
2 tablespoons tomato paste
1 (8-ounce) can diced tomatoes, drained
3 cups beef broth
1 cup long-grain white rice

1. Press the Sauté button on an Instant Pot® and allow to heat until the display reads "Hot." Place beef in the pot and use a wooden spoon to break into pieces. Brown until no pink remains, about 7 minutes.

2. Drain grease from the pot, then add salt, thyme, garlic powder, pepper, and onion to the pot. Sauté 2 minutes until onion begins to soften. Add cabbage, tomato paste, diced tomatoes, broth, and rice to the pot and stir to combine. Press the Cancel button.

3. Place the lid on the Instant Pot® and click into place to close. Press the Pressure Cook button and adjust the timer to 3 minutes. When the timer beeps, let the pressure release naturally for 10 minutes, then quick-release any remaining pressure until float valve drops. Unlock lid. Serve warm.

PER SERVING:

CALORIES: 285 | FAT: 8g | SODIUM: 985mg | CARBOHYDRATES: 34g | FIBER: 4g | SUGAR: 5g | PROTEIN: 17g

Green Enchilada Chicken Soup

Green enchilada sauce is made from green chiles rather than the typical red. Often you may see green enchilada sauce made with poblano peppers. Green enchilada sauce is mild and offers a fresher flavor than red enchilada sauce, which tends to be smoky and have a deeper flavor.

Hands-On Time: 10 minutes
Cook Time: 15 minutes

Serves 6

2 tablespoons olive oil
1 tablespoon salted butter
1 pound boneless, skinless chicken thighs, cut into 1" cubes
1 teaspoon salt
¼ teaspoon ground black pepper
½ teaspoon garlic powder
1 medium yellow onion, peeled and diced
1 (4-ounce) can green chiles, drained
1 (4-ounce) can diced tomatoes and green chiles, drained
¼ cup pickled jalapeños
1 cup green enchilada sauce
3 cups chicken broth
4 ounces cream cheese, cubed
1 cup long-grain white rice

1 Press the Sauté button on an Instant Pot® and allow to heat until the display reads "Hot." Add olive oil, butter, and chicken to the pot, then sprinkle with salt, pepper, and garlic powder. Sauté chicken 10 minutes until golden brown and fully cooked to an internal temperature of at least 165°F. Add onion to the pot and sauté 2 minutes until soft.

2 Press the Cancel button. Add remaining ingredients to the pot and stir to combine. Use a wooden spoon to scrape any browned bits from the bottom. Place the lid on the Instant Pot® and click into place to close.

3 Press the Pressure Cook button and adjust the timer to 3 minutes. When the timer beeps, let the pressure release naturally for 15 minutes, then quick-release any remaining pressure until float valve drops. Unlock lid. Serve warm.

PER SERVING:

CALORIES: 367 | FAT: 16g | SODIUM: 1,286mg | CARBOHYDRATES: 33g | FIBER: 2g | SUGAR: 4g | PROTEIN: 19g

Steakhouse Potato Chowder

Imagine your favorite bowl of loaded mashed potatoes. That's this dish in chowder form! It's filled to the brim with soft chunks of potato and topped with all the delicious toppings, including cheese and chopped bacon. Some potatoes break during cooking, which makes the chowder super creamy. The sour cream adds acidity to this dish and brightens the flavors, so be sure not to skip it. You may even add an extra spoonful on top for serving.

Hands-On Time: 10 minutes
Cook Time: 13 minutes

Serves 6

4 slices bacon, chopped into ½" pieces
2 tablespoons salted butter
½ medium yellow onion, peeled and chopped
½ teaspoon dried thyme
½ teaspoon salt
¼ teaspoon ground black pepper
3 large russet potatoes, peeled and diced
32 ounces chicken broth
1 cup whole milk
½ cup full-fat sour cream
1 cup shredded sharp Cheddar cheese
2 scallions, trimmed and sliced

1 Press the Sauté button on an Instant Pot® and allow to heat until the display reads "Hot." Add bacon to pot and sauté until browned, about 3 minutes. Add butter and onion and stir frequently until onion begins to soften, about 1 minute.

2 Add thyme, salt, and pepper to the pot. Add potatoes. Pour in broth, then use a wooden spoon to scrape the browned bits from the bottom. Place the lid on the Instant Pot® and click into place to close. Press the Cancel button. then press the Pressure Cook button and adjust the timer to 9 minutes.

3 When the timer beeps, quick-release the pressure until float valve drops. Unlock lid. Stir in milk and sour cream until well combined. Serve warm with Cheddar and scallions sprinkled on top.

PER SERVING:

CALORIES: 351 | **FAT**: 16g | **SODIUM**: 1,124mg | **CARBOHYDRATES**: 35g | **FIBER**: 3g | **SUGAR**: 5g | **PROTEIN**: 13g

Tuscan Soup

This is a popular soup that's delicious year-round. It's comforting with its creamy bites of potato, but is also light enough to accompany a salad or sandwich for a complete meal. This recipe uses kale, but if that's too bitter for your liking, feel free to swap with an equal amount of spinach.

Hands-On Time: 5 minutes
Cook Time: 23 minutes 30 seconds

Serves 6

1 pound Italian sausage
4 slices bacon, chopped
½ medium yellow onion, peeled and chopped
2 cloves garlic, peeled and minced
1 cup chopped kale
2 medium russet potatoes, peeled and diced
32 ounces chicken broth
1 teaspoon salt
¼ teaspoon ground black pepper
¼ cup heavy whipping cream
2 tablespoons cornstarch

1 Press the Sauté button on an Instant Pot® and allow to heat until the display reads "Hot." Crumble sausage and add it to the pot, then add bacon. Sauté until no pink remains and sausage and bacon are cooked through, about 8 minutes. Drain grease and return the pot to the base. Add onion and sauté 2 minutes, then add garlic and sauté 30 seconds.

2 Press the Cancel button. Add kale, potatoes, broth, salt, and pepper to the pot. Use a wooden spoon to scrape any browned pieces from the bottom. Place the lid on the Instant Pot® and click into place to close. Press the Pressure Cook button and adjust the timer to 8 minutes. When the timer beeps, quick-release the pressure until float valve drops. Unlock lid.

3 In a small bowl, whisk together cream and cornstarch. Press the Cancel button, then the Sauté button. Stir in cream mixture and cook while on Keep Warm mode 5 minutes to thicken soup. When soup is done, potatoes should be fork-tender. Serve warm.

PER SERVING:

CALORIES: 318 | FAT: 19g | SODIUM: 1,751mg | CARBOHYDRATES: 18g | FIBER: 1g | SUGAR: 2g | PROTEIN: 15g

Creamy Chipotle Chicken Soup

Each bite of this smoky chicken soup is packed with flavor. The protein and rice make this a filling dish, and it comes together in no time. This recipe doubles up on chipotle flavor by using chipotle powder and chipotle peppers in adobo sauce for maximum flavor. You can often find chipotle peppers in adobo sauce in the international food aisle in grocery stores.

Hands-On Time: 10 minutes
Cook Time: 5 minutes 30 seconds

Serves 6

2 tablespoons olive oil
1 medium yellow onion, peeled and chopped
2 cloves garlic, peeled and minced
2 teaspoons ground chili powder
1 teaspoon ground cumin
½ teaspoon smoked paprika
½ teaspoon chipotle powder
2 tablespoons tomato paste
1 (14.5-ounce) can diced tomatoes, drained
½ cup chipotles in adobo sauce, puréed
32 ounces chicken broth
3 cups shredded cooked chicken breasts
½ cup long-grain white rice, rinsed and drained
1 teaspoon salt
4 ounces cream cheese, softened
¾ cup shredded Cheddar cheese
6 tablespoons sour cream
2 tablespoons chopped fresh cilantro

1 Press the Sauté button on an Instant Pot® and allow to heat until the display reads "Hot." Add olive oil and onion to the pot. Sauté 2 minutes until onion softens. Add garlic, chili powder, cumin, paprika, chipotle powder, and tomato paste. Sauté 30 seconds until fragrant, then pour in diced tomatoes, chipotles in adobo sauce, and broth.

2 Press the Cancel button. Use a wooden spoon to scrape any browned bits from the bottom of the pot. Add chicken, rice, and salt. Place the lid on the Instant Pot® and click into place to close. Press the Pressure Cook button and adjust the timer to 3 minutes. When the timer beeps, let the pressure release naturally for 10 minutes until float valve drops. Unlock lid.

3 Whisk cream cheese into the pot until melted and smooth. Serve warm, topped with Cheddar and sour cream. Garnish with cilantro. Serve warm.

PER SERVING:

CALORIES: 410 | FAT: 19g | SODIUM: 1,502mg | CARBOHYDRATES: 23g | FIBER: 3g | SUGAR: 5g | PROTEIN: 30g

Tomato Lentil Soup

Lentils are a great way to get some extra fiber into your soup. They're a legume, and when cooked, they're tender, almost like a grain. They have a mild taste, which makes them a great addition to just about any soup. This soup is packed with vegetables, making it something you can feel good about eating.

Hands-On Time: 10 minutes
Cook Time: 12 minutes 30 seconds

Serves 6

- 2 tablespoons olive oil
- ½ medium yellow onion, peeled and diced
- 2 medium stalks celery, trimmed and diced
- 1 large carrot, peeled and diced
- 1 teaspoon salt
- 1 teaspoon ground cumin
- ½ teaspoon ground chili powder
- ¼ teaspoon garlic powder
- 2 tablespoons tomato paste
- 1 (8-ounce) can tomato sauce
- 1 (14.5-ounce) can diced tomatoes, drained
- 1 cup brown lentils
- 4 cups vegetable broth
- 2 cups water

1 Press the Sauté button on an Instant Pot® and allow to heat until the display reads "Hot." Add olive oil, onion, celery, and carrot. Sauté 2 minutes until vegetables begin to soften.

2 Add salt, cumin, chili powder, garlic powder, tomato paste, and tomato sauce. Sauté 30 seconds, then press the Cancel button. Pour in tomatoes and lentils. Use a wooden spoon to scrape any browned bits from the bottom and stir. Pour in broth and water.

3 Place the lid on the Instant Pot® and click into place to close. Press the Pressure Cook button and adjust the timer to 10 minutes. When the timer beeps, let the pressure release naturally for 15 minutes until float valve drops. Unlock lid. When soup is done, lentils will be soft. Serve warm.

PER SERVING:

CALORIES: 217 | **FAT:** 6g | **SODIUM:** 1,212mg | **CARBOHYDRATES:** 31g | **FIBER:** 6g | **SUGAR:** 7g | **PROTEIN:** 10g

4

Rice, Beans, and Pasta

The Instant Pot® completely changes the way you prepare rice, beans, and pasta—speeding up and simplifying the process forever. These grains are not only delicious, but they're also all part of a healthy, well-rounded diet. Taking the guesswork out of your spaghetti and serving it up quicker means more time around the dinner table, enjoying a meal with your loved ones. With such recipes as Cheeseburger Macaroni, Creamy Lemon Orzo, and plenty of flavorful beans, this chapter is full of delicious and family-friendly recipes to incorporate into your meal rotation!

Risotto 52

Cilantro Lime Rice 53

Mushroom Wild Rice 54

Long-Grain White Rice 54

Cajun-Style Rice 55

Quick Chicken Steamed Rice 56

Mexican-Style Rice 58

Pinto Beans 59

Black Beans 60

Creamy Alfredo Penne 60

Baked Beans 61

Pesto Feta Pasta 63

Chickpeas 64

Creamy Lemon Orzo 64

Spaghetti 65

Carbonara 66

Quick and Easy Penne 67

Buttery Egg Noodles 67

Spinach and Cheese Manicotti 68

Cheeseburger Macaroni 70

Risotto

Creamy risotto is now easier than ever! Typically, risotto can be time-consuming and require a lot of stirring. With the Instant Pot®, you can enjoy super creamy risotto in record time with little effort. This recipe uses Arborio rice, a common type of short-grain rice that's easy to find. Arborio rice is high in starch, which is what makes this dish creamy, so no substitutions will work in this recipe.

Hands-On Time: 5 minutes
Cook Time: 8 minutes 30 seconds

Serves 8

2 tablespoons salted butter
½ medium yellow onion, peeled and finely chopped
2 cloves garlic, peeled and finely minced
1½ cups Arborio rice
3 cups chicken broth
½ teaspoon salt
¼ teaspoon ground black pepper
½ cup grated Parmesan cheese

1 Press the Sauté button on an Instant Pot® and allow to heat until the display reads "Hot." Place butter and onion in the pot. Sauté 2 minutes until onion softens. Add garlic and rice and sauté 30 seconds to toast rice.

2 Pour broth into the pot and stir. Sprinkle with salt and pepper. Place the lid on the Instant Pot® and click into place to close. Press the Pressure Cook button and adjust the timer to 6 minutes. When the timer beeps, quick-release the pressure until float valve drops. Unlock lid.

3 Stir in Parmesan until well combined and risotto is creamy. Serve warm.

PER SERVING:

CALORIES: 195 | FAT: 4g | SODIUM: 627mg | CARBOHYDRATES: 32g | FIBER: 1g | SUGAR: 1g | PROTEIN: 5g

Cilantro Lime Rice

If you've ever doubted your ability to make rice, the Instant Pot® can help you execute perfectly fluffy rice every time without any fuss. To easily reheat this rice and keep it fluffy, microwave it in a bowl sprinkled with 1 tablespoon water and covered with a plate (leaving a small amount of space to vent) for 3 minutes. Fluff with a fork.

Hands-On Time: 5 minutes
Cook Time: 3 minutes

Serves 4

1 cup long-grain rice, rinsed and drained
1 tablespoon lime juice
1 cup water
½ teaspoon olive oil
½ teaspoon salt
4 tablespoons finely chopped fresh cilantro, divided
1 teaspoon grated lime zest

1   Place rice, lime juice, water, olive oil, salt, and 2 tablespoons cilantro in an Instant Pot®.

2   Place the lid on the pot and click into place to close. Press the Pressure Cook button and adjust the timer to 3 minutes. When the timer beeps, let the pressure release naturally for 10 minutes, then quick-release any remaining pressure until float valve drops. Unlock lid.

3   Fluff rice with a fork, then sprinkle with lime zest and remaining 2 tablespoons cilantro. Serve warm.

PER SERVING:

CALORIES: 174 | FAT: 1g | SODIUM: 293mg | CARBOHYDRATES: 37g | FIBER: 1g | SUGAR: 0g | PROTEIN: 3g

Mushroom Wild Rice

Wild rice blend is a more textured blend of rice and can elevate any dish and add lots of flavor.

Hands-On Time: 5 minutes
Cook Time: 32 minutes

Serves 6

1 tablespoon olive oil
½ medium white onion, peeled and chopped
1 cup chopped cremini mushrooms
¼ teaspoon salt
2 cups water
1 cup wild rice blend, rinsed and drained

1 Press the Sauté button on an Instant Pot® and allow to heat until the display reads "Hot." Add olive oil, onion, mushrooms, and salt to the pot. Sauté 2 minutes until vegetables begin to soften. Press the Cancel button.

2 Add water and rice to the pot and stir. Place the lid on the Instant Pot® and click into place to close. Press the Pressure Cook button and adjust the timer to 30 minutes.

3 When the timer beeps, quick-release the pressure until float valve drops. Unlock lid. Fluff rice with a fork and serve warm.

PER SERVING:

CALORIES: 121 | **FAT:** 2g | **SODIUM:** 99mg | **CARBOHYDRATES:** 21g | **FIBER:** 2g | **SUGAR:** 1g | **PROTEIN:** 4g

Long-Grain White Rice

The Instant Pot® can function like a rice cooker and give you perfectly fluffy rice every time you make it.

Hands-On Time: 5 minutes
Cook Time: 3 minutes

Serves 6

1 cup long-grain white rice, rinsed and drained
1 cup water
½ teaspoon salt

1 Place all ingredients in an Instant Pot®. Place the lid on the Instant Pot® and click into place to close.

2 Press the Pressure Cook button and adjust the timer to 3 minutes. When the timer beeps, let the pressure release naturally for 10 minutes, then quick-release any remaining pressure until float valve drops. Unlock lid.

3 Fluff rice with a fork. Serve warm.

PER SERVING:

CALORIES: 102 | **FAT:** 0g | **SODIUM:** 194mg | **CARBOHYDRATES:** 22g | **FIBER:** 0g | **SUGAR:** 0g | **PROTEIN:** 2g

Cajun-Style Rice

This rice is so delicious; it can be a side or the main dish. It's packed with flavor, but it won't set you back on time. Feel free to add 1 teaspoon of your favorite Cajun seasoning to this dish. The fluffy rice and tender vegetables go well with chicken or even smoked sausage. If you have leftover beans from another recipe, you can also add ½ cup of them to this dish.

Hands-On Time: 10 minutes
Cook Time: 6 minutes

Serves 8

2 tablespoons salted butter
½ medium white onion, peeled and chopped
¼ cup chopped celery
½ medium red bell pepper, seeded and chopped
¼ teaspoon smoked paprika
½ teaspoon salt
¼ teaspoon ground black pepper
1 cup long-grain white rice, rinsed and drained
½ cup tomato sauce
2 cups chicken broth

1 Press the Sauté button on an Instant Pot® and allow to heat until the display reads "Hot." Add butter, onion, celery, and bell pepper. Sauté 3 minutes until vegetables begin to soften. Add paprika, salt, and black pepper to the pot and stir to combine. Pour in rice, tomato sauce, and broth. Stir, then press the Cancel button.

2 Place the lid on the Instant Pot® and click into place to close. Press the Pressure Cook button and adjust the timer to 3 minutes. When the timer beeps, let the pressure release naturally for 10 minutes, then quick-release any remaining pressure until float valve drops. Unlock lid.

3 When done, rice should be soft, and red in color. Fluff rice with a fork. Serve warm.

PER SERVING:

CALORIES: 126 | FAT: 3g | SODIUM: 455mg | CARBOHYDRATES: 20g | FIBER: 1g | SUGAR: 1g | PROTEIN: 2g

Quick Chicken Steamed Rice

This easy dish is inspired by fried rice. For fried rice, you typically need to cook the rice first and allow it to fully chill before frying for best results. This recipe allows the whole recipe to be cooked at once and uses less oil than you would with frying. It's softer than typical fried rice but still has all the flavors you love, and it's ready in 30 minutes.

Hands-On Time: 10 minutes
Cook Time: 10 minutes

Serves 6

2 tablespoons refined coconut oil
1 pound boneless, skinless chicken breasts, cut into ½" cubes
½ teaspoon salt
¼ teaspoon ground black pepper
2 cups chicken broth
1 cup long-grain white rice, rinsed and drained
¼ cup low-sodium soy sauce
½ cup frozen diced carrots
1 cup frozen broccoli florets
2 scallions, trimmed and sliced

1 Press the Sauté button on an Instant Pot® and allow to heat until the display reads "Hot." Pour oil into the pot. Season both sides of chicken with salt and pepper, then add to the pot and sauté 7 minutes until chicken is golden brown and the internal temperature is at least 165°F.

2 Press the Cancel button. Pour broth into the pot, then use a wooden spoon to scrape any browned bits from the bottom. Add rice, soy sauce, carrots, and broccoli. Place the lid on the Instant Pot® and click into place to close. Press the Pressure Cook button and adjust the timer to 3 minutes. When the timer beeps, let the pressure release naturally for 10 minutes, then quick-release any remaining pressure until float valve drops. Unlock lid.

3 Fluff rice with a fork and top with scallions. Serve warm.

PER SERVING:

CALORIES: 253 | FAT: 6g | SODIUM: 822mg | CARBOHYDRATES: 29g | FIBER: 2g | SUGAR: 2g | PROTEIN: 20g

Mexican-Style Rice

This side is a flavorful addition to many meals. The rice becomes red in color and has lots of flavor from the spices. The key to extra flavor in this dish is sautéing the spices before you add the liquid. It allows the aromatics to develop and the flavors to release before the real cooking begins. Try this rice with a little sour cream and chopped Roma tomatoes on top.

Hands-On Time: 15 minutes
Cook Time: 6 minutes

Serves 6

1 tablespoon olive oil
½ medium yellow onion, peeled and chopped
1 cup long-grain white rice, rinsed, drained, and dried
½ tablespoon chili powder
1 teaspoon ground cumin
½ teaspoon salt
1 tablespoon tomato paste
8 ounces tomato sauce
1 cup water
2 tablespoons chopped fresh cilantro

DRY RICE

This recipe is unique in that it calls for rinsed, drained, and dried rice. Toasting the rice adds flavor to this recipe and is worth the extra step. But before it's toasted, the starch must be rinsed off. Once you rinse the rice, leave it in the colander for 10 minutes and it will be dried. The drying time has been included in the prep time.

1. Press the Sauté button on an Instant Pot® and allow to heat until the display reads "Hot." Add olive oil and onion to the pot and sauté 2 minutes until onion begins to soften.

2. Add rice, chili powder, cumin, and salt to the pot. Sauté 1 minute until fragrant, stirring frequently. Add tomato paste. Press the Cancel button.

3. Pour tomato sauce and water into the pot. Place the lid on the Instant Pot® and click into place to close. Press the Pressure Cook button and adjust the timer to 3 minutes. When the timer beeps, let the pressure release naturally for 10 minutes, then quick-release any remaining pressure until float valve drops. Unlock lid. Fluff rice with a fork and sprinkle with cilantro. Serve warm.

PER SERVING:

CALORIES: 166 | FAT: 4g | SODIUM: 363mg | CARBOHYDRATES: 28g | FIBER: 1g | SUGAR: 2g | PROTEIN: 3g

Pinto Beans

Canned beans are convenient but can sometimes have a lot of added sodium. When you cook dry beans, it's easier to control the amount of salt. Plus, you can add other spices to build flavor. Typically, dry beans might be off-putting because of their long cook time, but the Instant Pot® makes it easier than ever. In less than an hour, you have a pot of seasoned beans to enjoy as a side dish or to add to soups or burritos.

Hands-On Time: 10 minutes
Cook Time: 35 minutes

Serves 16

- 1 pound dry pinto beans, rinsed and debris removed
- 1 medium yellow onion, peeled and diced
- 1 small jalapeño, seeded and sliced
- 1 tablespoon chili powder
- 2 teaspoons ground cumin
- 1 teaspoon salt
- ¼ teaspoon ground black pepper
- 5 cups water

1 Place all ingredients in an Instant Pot® and mix until well combined.

2 Place the lid on the Instant Pot® and click into place to close. Press the Pressure Cook button and adjust the timer to 35 minutes.

3 When the timer beeps, quick-release the pressure until float valve drops. Unlock lid. Stir beans and serve warm.

PER SERVING:

CALORIES: 104 | FAT: 0g | SODIUM: 163mg | CARBOHYDRATES: 19g | FIBER: 5g | SUGAR: 1g | PROTEIN: 6g

SORTING

It's important to sort through your beans before rinsing them. Sometimes small pieces of gravel or dirt get mixed into the bag. This is also a time to inspect the beans and remove any that are damaged or look irregular.

Black Beans

Black beans are denser than pinto beans, so if you've never tried them, you will be pleasantly surprised at how tender and flavorful these protein-filled beans really can be.

Hands-On Time: 5 minutes
Cook Time: 30 minutes

Serves 6

1 cup dry black beans, rinsed and debris removed
1 cup vegetable broth
2 cups water
¼ cup lime juice
1 teaspoon chili powder
1 teaspoon ground cumin
1 teaspoon salt
½ teaspoon garlic powder
¼ teaspoon ground black pepper

1 Place all ingredients in an Instant Pot® and stir to combine.

2 Place the lid on the Instant Pot® and click into place to close. Press the Pressure Cook button and adjust the timer to 30 minutes. When the timer beeps, let the pressure release naturally for 20 minutes, then quick-release any remaining pressure until float valve drops. Unlock lid.

3 Stir beans. Serve warm.

PER SERVING:

CALORIES: 118 | FAT: 0g | SODIUM: 536mg | CARBOHYDRATES: 22g | FIBER: 5g | SUGAR: 1g | PROTEIN: 7g

Creamy Alfredo Penne

This delicious meal is full of cheesy, creamy sauce. Enjoy this dish as is, or top it with cooked chicken and broccoli for a well-rounded dinner.

Hands-On Time: 5 minutes
Cook Time: 5 minutes

Serves 4

2 cups uncooked penne pasta
2 cups chicken broth
½ teaspoon salt
2 tablespoons salted butter, cubed
¼ cup heavy whipping cream
½ cup grated Parmesan cheese
2 ounces cream cheese, softened

1 Place penne, broth, salt, and butter in an Instant Pot® and stir. Place the lid on the Instant Pot® and click into place to close. Press the Pressure Cook button and adjust the timer to 5 minutes.

2 When the timer beeps, quick-release the pressure until float valve drops. Unlock lid.

3 Stir in cream, Parmesan, and cream cheese until fully melted and creamy. Serve warm.

PER SERVING:

CALORIES: 630 | FAT: 19g | SODIUM: 1,087mg | CARBOHYDRATES: 88g | FIBER: 4g | SUGAR: 4g | PROTEIN: 20g

Baked Beans

This perfectly sauced-up dish is the ultimate side for your next barbecue. If you love baked beans and never took the time to make homemade, this recipe will be your new favorite. The sauce is sweet and rich, and the beans are soft. This recipe uses great northern beans, but you can substitute an equal amount of navy beans if you prefer.

Hands-On Time: 5 minutes
Cook Time: 46 minutes

Serves 8

4 slices bacon, chopped
½ medium yellow onion, peeled and diced
1 cup cooked great northern beans
6 tablespoons ketchup
¼ cup molasses
5 tablespoons dark brown sugar, packed
1 teaspoon yellow mustard
2 teaspoons Worcestershire sauce
½ teaspoon liquid smoke
1 cup water

1 Press the Sauté button on an Instant Pot® and allow to heat until the display reads "Hot." Add bacon to the pot and sauté until fully cooked and browned, about 5 minutes. Add onion and sauté until fragrant, about 1 minute. Add remaining ingredients and stir. Press the Cancel button.

2 Place the lid on the Instant Pot® and click into place to close. Press the Pressure Cook button and adjust the timer to 35 minutes. When the timer beeps, let the pressure release naturally for 10 minutes, then quick-release any remaining pressure until float valve drops. Unlock lid.

3 Press the Cancel button, then the Sauté button. Sauté 5 minutes to allow mixture to reduce and thicken. Serve warm.

PER SERVING:

CALORIES: 164 | FAT: 5g | SODIUM: 236mg | CARBOHYDRATES: 26g | FIBER: 2g | SUGAR: 20g | PROTEIN: 4g

Pesto Feta Pasta

When heated, the feta in this recipe turns into a creamy sauce that coats the pasta, with no actual cream needed. This light red sauce has just the right amount of tang from the pesto. If you're a fan of pesto, this recipe is a must-try. Add a sprinkle of crushed red pepper if you want a little heat.

Hands-On Time: 5 minutes
Cook Time: 5 minutes

Serves 4

1½ cups vegetable broth
½ cup basil pesto
2 cups uncooked penne pasta
8 ounces feta cheese
1 teaspoon salt
2 teaspoons Italian seasoning
1 cup grape tomatoes
1 tablespoon olive oil
¼ cup sliced fresh basil

1 Place broth, pesto, and penne in an Instant Pot®. Sprinkle in feta, salt, and Italian seasoning. Place grape tomatoes in the pot and drizzle with olive oil. Place the lid on the Instant Pot® and click into place to close. Press the Pressure Cook button and adjust the timer to 5 minutes. When the timer beeps, quick-release the pressure until float valve drops. Unlock lid.

2 Use a wooden spoon to stir pasta mixture quickly so that a creamy sauce forms. Top with basil. Serve warm.

PER SERVING:

CALORIES: 467 | FAT: 27g | SODIUM: 1,685mg | CARBOHYDRATES: 39g | FIBER: 2g | SUGAR: 6g | PROTEIN: 15g

Chickpeas

This recipe is excellent to have on hand to use in Taco Soup (see recipe in Chapter 3)!

Hands-On Time: 5 minutes
Cook Time: 50 minutes

Serves 4

2 cups dry chickpeas, rinsed and debris removed
1 teaspoon salt
5 cups water

1 Place all ingredients in an Instant Pot®. Place the lid on the Instant Pot® and click into place to close.

2 Press the Pressure Cook button and adjust the timer to 50 minutes.

3 When the timer beeps, let the pressure release naturally for 15 minutes, then quick-release any remaining pressure until float valve drops. Unlock lid. When done, a chickpea should be easily mashed with a fork. Serve warm.

PER SERVING:

CALORIES: 378 | FAT: 5g | SODIUM: 605mg | CARBOHYDRATES: 63g | FIBER: 12g | SUGAR: 11g | PROTEIN: 20g

Creamy Lemon Orzo

Orzo looks similar to short-grain rice but is actually pasta. It's delicious by itself or alongside your main protein. This dish is light and fresh, making it a great choice to enjoy in the summer.

Hands-On Time: 5 minutes
Cook Time: 6 minutes

Serves 6

2 tablespoons salted butter
1 tablespoon grated lemon zest
½ teaspoon salt
¼ teaspoon ground black pepper
1½ cups uncooked orzo
1½ cups vegetable broth
3 tablespoons lemon juice
¼ cup heavy whipping cream
½ cup grated Parmesan cheese

1 Press the Sauté button on an Instant Pot® and allow to heat until the display reads "Hot." Add butter, lemon zest, salt, pepper, and orzo to the pot. Sauté 1 minute, then press the Cancel button.

2 Pour broth and lemon juice into the pot. Place the lid on the Instant Pot® and click into place to close. Press the Pressure Cook button and adjust the timer to 5 minutes. When the timer beeps, quick-release the pressure until float valve drops. Unlock lid.

3 Stir in cream and Parmesan. Serve warm.

PER SERVING:

CALORIES: 257 | FAT: 10g | SODIUM: 578mg | CARBOHYDRATES: 34g | FIBER: 2g | SUGAR: 2g | PROTEIN: 8g

Spaghetti

This classic weeknight dinner just got even easier when you don't have to wait for water to boil on the stove. With the Instant Pot®, you can just put in all the ingredients and take care of something else, such as preparing a side salad or warm garlic bread.

Hands-On Time: 5 minutes
Cook Time: 10 minutes

Serves 4

2 cups water
2 tablespoons tomato paste
16 ounces uncooked spaghetti
3 cups pasta sauce
½ teaspoon salt
1 teaspoon Italian seasoning
¼ teaspoon garlic powder
½ cup grated Parmesan cheese

FROZEN MEATBALLS

If you're a fan of meatballs, simply add a steamer basket to the pot after all spaghetti ingredients are in the pot. Place the frozen meatballs in the basket and keep the same cook time. They will steam to perfection while the spaghetti is cooked, then you can stir in or place on top to serve.

1 Pour water in an Instant Pot® and whisk in tomato paste. Break spaghetti in half and fan out on top of water, then pour sauce over spaghetti. Sprinkle salt, Italian seasoning, and garlic powder over sauce. (Do not stir. Stirring will make the pasta stick together.)

2 Place the lid on the Instant Pot® and click into place to close. Press the Pressure Cook button and adjust the timer to 10 minutes. When the timer beeps, quick-release the pressure until float valve drops. Unlock lid.

3 Stir spaghetti and stir in Parmesan. Serve warm.

PER SERVING:

CALORIES: 563 | FAT: 6g | SODIUM: 1,298mg | CARBOHYDRATES: 101g | FIBER: 7g | SUGAR: 13g | PROTEIN: 21g

Carbonara

This dish is perfect for last-minute meals. Whether you're looking for something new or you're in a pinch and don't have any pasta sauce, this recipe might just become a new favorite. Each bite is full of a rich and creamy Parmesan sauce that's made right in the pot.

Hands-On Time: 5 minutes
Cook Time: 11 minutes 30 seconds

Serves 4

4 slices bacon, chopped
1 medium yellow onion, peeled and finely diced
1 clove garlic, peeled and finely minced
2 cups chicken broth
16 ounces uncooked spaghetti, broken in half
1 teaspoon salt
¼ teaspoon ground black pepper
2 large egg yolks, room temperature
2 cups grated Parmesan cheese
¼ cup heavy cream

ROOM-TEMPERATURE EGGS
Using room-temperature eggs in this recipe helps prevent clumps from forming in your sauce. Usually this takes about 30 minutes when the eggs sit on the counter. If you're in a rush, you can warm them quickly by placing the whole eggs in a cup of warm tap water. Within 5–10 minutes the shells should no longer feel cold and they will be ready to use.

1 Press the Sauté button on an Instant Pot® and allow to heat until the display reads "Hot." Place bacon in the pot and cook until crispy, about 4 minutes. Add onion and sauté 2 minutes until it begins to soften, then add garlic and sauté 30 seconds. Pour in broth and use a wooden spoon to scrape the browned bits from the bottom of the pot and stir.

2 Press the Cancel button. Add spaghetti to the pot and sprinkle with salt and pepper. Do not stir. Place the lid on the Instant Pot® and click into place to close. Press the Pressure Cook button and adjust the timer to 5 minutes. When the timer beeps, quick-release the pressure until float valve drops. Unlock lid.

3 Press the Cancel button. While pasta is still hot, slowly pour in egg yolks and stir quickly until fully combined, then add Parmesan and cream. A thick sauce will form; stir to coat spaghetti in sauce. Serve warm.

PER SERVING:

CALORIES: 845 | FAT: 31g | SODIUM: 2,147mg | CARBOHYDRATES: 96g | FIBER: 4g | SUGAR: 6g | PROTEIN: 35g

Quick and Easy Penne

Most dry pasta will cook in 5 minutes, so feel free to switch up the penne in this recipe. Elbow macaroni, spaghetti, and bow ties are all excellent choices with the same cook time.

Hands-On Time: 5 minutes
Cook Time: 5 minutes

Serves 4

2 cups water
2 cups uncooked penne pasta
1 teaspoon salt
1 tablespoon olive oil

1 Pour water into an Instant Pot® and then add penne. Sprinkle salt on top.

2 Place the lid on the Instant Pot® and click into place to close. Press the Pressure Cook button and adjust the timer to 5 minutes.

3 When the timer beeps, quick-release the pressure until float valve drops. Unlock lid. Drizzle with olive oil. Serve warm.

PER SERVING:

CALORIES: 450 | **FAT:** 4g | **SODIUM:** 588mg | **CARBOHYDRATES:** 85g | **FIBER:** 4g | **SUGAR:** 3g | **PROTEIN:** 15g

Buttery Egg Noodles

Egg noodles are thinner than most dry pasta and cook up in just a couple of minutes! Whether you're making a plate of simple buttered noodles or a batch of beef Stroganoff, this recipe will ensure your noodles come out perfect every time.

Hands-On Time: 5 minutes
Cook Time: 2 minutes

Serves 4

16 ounces uncooked egg noodles
2 cups water
1 teaspoon salt
2 tablespoons salted butter
2 tablespoons dried parsley

1 Place noodles, water, and salt in an Instant Pot® and stir to combine.

2 Place the lid on the Instant Pot® and click into place to close. Press the Pressure Cook button and adjust the timer to 2 minutes.

3 When the timer beeps, quick-release the pressure until float valve drops. Unlock lid. Stir in butter until fully melted. Sprinkle with parsley. Serve warm.

PER SERVING:

CALORIES: 478 | **FAT:** 10g | **SODIUM:** 640mg | **CARBOHYDRATES:** 77g | **FIBER:** 4g | **SUGAR:** 4g | **PROTEIN:** 16g

Spinach and Cheese Manicotti

This classic meal is now easier than ever with an Instant Pot®. Rather than cooking your pasta separately and then adding the filling, you can simply add the filling before the pasta is cooked. The Instant Pot® steams the manicotti to perfection and cooks the delicious cheese and spinach filling at the same time, so your meal is ready in less time and with less fuss.

Hands-On Time: 10 minutes
Cook Time: 8 minutes

Serves 4

½ cup full-fat ricotta cheese
1 cup shredded mozzarella cheese, divided
¼ cup grated Parmesan cheese
1 large egg
1 cup chopped baby spinach
1 teaspoon Italian seasoning
¾ teaspoon salt
¼ teaspoon ground black pepper
¼ teaspoon garlic powder
8 ounces uncooked manicotti
½ cup vegetable broth
3 cups marinara sauce

1 In a large bowl, mix ricotta, ½ cup mozzarella, and Parmesan until smooth. Mix in egg, spinach, Italian seasoning, salt, pepper, and garlic powder until well combined.

2 Place mixture in a piping bag and cut 1" off the end of the bag. Pipe mixture into manicotti. Pour broth and 1 cup marinara sauce into an Instant Pot®. Place half of manicotti in the pot, then 1 cup marinara sauce. Add remaining manicotti, then remaining 1 cup marinara sauce, and top with remaining ½ cup mozzarella.

3 Place the lid on the pot and click into place to close. Press the Pressure Cook button and adjust the timer to 8 minutes. When the timer beeps, quick-release the pressure until float valve drops. Unlock lid. Serve warm.

PER SERVING:

CALORIES: 460 | **FAT:** 12g | **SODIUM:** 1,560mg | **CARBOHYDRATES:** 60g | **FIBER:** 5g | **SUGAR:** 12g | **PROTEIN:** 22g

Cheeseburger Macaroni

This dish is going to be a weeknight staple! If you love Hamburger Helper, then this home-made version is for you. The whole family will enjoy this creamy, cheesy pasta dish. You'll be impressed with how perfectly all the flavors come together in this quick-cooking meal.

Hands-On Time: 10 minutes
Cook Time: 12 minutes

Serves 6

1 pound 70/30 ground beef
½ medium yellow onion, peeled and diced
1 tablespoon tomato paste
2 cups chicken broth
½ teaspoon salt
¼ teaspoon ground black pepper
2 cups uncooked elbow macaroni
1 cup shredded medium Cheddar cheese
¼ cup whole milk

TACO SEASONING

To change up the flavor of this meal, add a packet of taco seasoning with the broth and leave out the salt listed in this recipe. You can even top the dish with crushed tortilla chips for some crunch.

1 Press the Sauté button on an Instant Pot® and allow to heat until the display reads "Hot." Using a wooden spoon, break beef into pieces and sauté 7 minutes until no pink remains. Add onion, tomato paste, and broth to the pot. Scrape the bottom with a wooden spoon to remove any browned bits.

2 Add salt, pepper, and macaroni and stir to combine. Press the Cancel button. Place the lid on the Instant Pot® and click into place to close. Press the Pressure Cook button and adjust the timer to 5 minutes. When the timer beeps, quick-release the pressure until float valve drops. Unlock lid.

3 Stir in Cheddar and milk until smooth. Serve warm.

PER SERVING:

CALORIES: 474 | FAT: 26g | SODIUM: 700mg | CARBOHYDRATES: 29g | FIBER: 1g | SUGAR: 3g | PROTEIN: 21g

Appetizers and Snacks

Whether they're for a game-day party, potluck, or after-school treat, everybody loves appetizers and snacks. These scrumptious goodies are the perfect little bites for guests to enjoy over good conversations, or for simply holding you over between meals. If your Instant Pot® is invited to the party, you're sure to have a great time! From Buffalo Chicken Dip to Bacon and Cream Cheese–Stuffed Mushrooms, this chapter's yummy recipes will get gobbled up as quickly as they are made.

Hard-Cooked Eggs 72

Buffalo Chicken Dip 73

Chili Cheese Dip 73

Slow Cooker Beefy Queso Dip 74

Ranch Slow Cooker Snack Mix 75

Spinach Artichoke Dip 77

Cajun Boiled Peanuts 78

Grape Jelly Meatballs 79

Barbecue Mini Smoked Sausages 80

Applesauce 80

Restaurant-Style Red Salsa 81

Spicy Chicken Sliders 82

Mini Greek Turkey Meatballs 84

Bacon and Cream Cheese–Stuffed Mushrooms 85

Barbecue Wings 86

Popcorn 87

Buffalo Chicken Wings 89

Hard-Cooked Eggs

These eggs are perfect for keeping in the refrigerator for when you need something quick and satisfying, but they're also great to take on the go. You can use this recipe anytime you wish you to make deviled eggs or egg salad. Be aware that some Instant Pot® models can heat differently, so try the first egg by itself and adjust the cook time to find what works best for your model.

Hands-On Time: 5 minutes
Cook Time: 8 minutes

Serves 8

1 cup water
8 large eggs

1 Pour water into an Instant Pot® and place the trivet in the pot, then place eggs on trivet. Place the lid on the Instant Pot® and click into place to close.

2 Press the Pressure Cook button and adjust the timer to 8 minutes. When the timer beeps, quick-release the pressure until float valve drops. Unlock lid.

3 Carefully place eggs in a large bowl of ice water to cool for at least 15 minutes. Eggs will keep in the refrigerator for up to 4 days. Peel before serving.

PER SERVING:

CALORIES: 77 | FAT: 4g | SODIUM: 62mg | CARBOHYDRATES: 1g | FIBER: 0g | SUGAR: 1g | PROTEIN: 6g

Buffalo Chicken Dip

Whether you dip tortilla chips or fresh carrots and celery, this recipe is sure to please. At parties, you can even leave it on the Keep Warm function for serving.

Hands-On Time: 10 minutes
Cook Time: 5 minutes

Serves 8

2 cups shredded cooked chicken breast

8 ounces cream cheese, softened

½ cup buffalo wing sauce

½ cup ranch dressing

½ cup chicken broth

1 (1-ounce) packet dry ranch seasoning

1 cup shredded sharp Cheddar cheese

1 Place chicken, cream cheese, wing sauce, ranch dressing, broth, and ranch seasoning in an Instant Pot®. Place the lid on the Instant Pot® and click into place to close.

2 Press the Pressure Cook button and adjust the timer to 5 minutes. When the timer beeps, quick-release the pressure until float valve drops. Unlock lid.

3 Stir in Cheddar until well combined. Serve warm.

PER SERVING:

CALORIES: 229 | **FAT:** 14g | **SODIUM:** 1,012mg | **CARBOHYDRATES:** 3g | **FIBER:** 0g | **SUGAR:** 1g | **PROTEIN:** 16g

Chili Cheese Dip

This classic party dip is now even easier to prepare. The canned chili makes it easy to put together, but feel free to make your own from scratch instead (see the Red Chili recipe in Chapter 3).

Hands-On Time: 5 minutes
Cook Time: 3 minutes

Serves 12

2 (8-ounce) cans beef and bean chili

1 (8-ounce) block processed American cheese, such as Kraft Velveeta, cut into cubes

4 ounces cream cheese, cubed

1 Place all ingredients in an Instant Pot®.

2 Place the lid on the Instant Pot® and click into place to close. Press the Pressure Cook button and adjust the timer to 3 minutes. When the timer beeps, quick-release the pressure until float valve drops. Unlock lid.

3 Stir dip to ensure all ingredients are well combined. Serve warm.

PER SERVING:

CALORIES: 131 | **FAT:** 7g | **SODIUM:** 514mg | **CARBOHYDRATES:** 7g | **FIBER:** 2g | **SUGAR:** 2g | **PROTEIN:** 6g

Slow Cooker Beefy Queso Dip

One of the great things about the Instant Pot® is that it includes many functions of other appliances, so you can condense your kitchen collection. The Slow Cook function is a great way to make a party dip because not only will it cook while you prepare everything else, it will also keep the food perfectly warm and ready to serve at any time. This dip features cheese and seasoned beef. Whether you dip your chips or pour this over them like nachos, this is sure to be a favorite.

Hands-On Time: 5 minutes
Cook Time: 4 hours 9 minutes

Serves 24

1 pound 90/10 ground beef
1 medium yellow onion, peeled and diced
1 (10-ounce) can diced tomatoes and green chiles
1 (16-ounce) block processed American cheese, such as Kraft Velveeta, cut into cubes

SHORT ON TIME?

You can pressure cook this recipe too. Place the lid on the Instant Pot® and click into place to close. Press the Pressure Cook button and adjust the timer to 3 minutes. When the timer beeps, quick-release the pressure until float valve drops. Unlock lid, stir until well combined, then serve warm.

1 Press the Sauté button on an Instant Pot® and allow to heat until the display reads "Hot." Break beef into pieces and add to the pot. Sauté until no pink remains and beef is crumbled, about 7 minutes. Add onion and sauté 2 minutes until softened. Press the Cancel button.

2 Add remaining ingredients to the pot and stir to combine. Place a glass slow cooker lid on the Instant Pot®. Press the Slow Cook button and adjust the timer to 4 hours.

3 Stir mixture once per hour. Serve warm.

PER SERVING:

CALORIES: 94 | FAT: 4g | SODIUM: 331mg | CARBOHYDRATES: 3g | FIBER: 0g | SUGAR: 2g | PROTEIN: 7g

Ranch Slow Cooker Snack Mix

This recipe is a classic, and the Slow Cook function on the Instant Pot® makes preparing it super easy. Every 30 minutes when the mixture needs to be stirred, you'll be glad you don't have to keep opening the oven and taking a baking sheet out to stir.

Hands-On Time: 5 minutes
Cook Time: 3 hours

Serves 10

2 cups Corn Chex cereal
2 cups Rice Chex cereal
2 cups cheese crackers
2 cups pretzel sticks
½ cup salted butter, melted
2 tablespoons Worcestershire sauce
1 (1-ounce) packet dry ranch seasoning

1 Place both cereals, crackers, and pretzels in an Instant Pot®. In a small bowl, whisk butter, Worcestershire sauce, and ranch seasoning. Pour mixture into the Instant Pot® and stir to coat all ingredients.

2 Place a glass slow cooker lid on the Instant Pot®. Press the Slow Cook button, set to "Less," and adjust the timer to 3 hours. Stir mixture every 30 minutes.

3 Spread snack mix in an even layer on two large baking sheets. The mix may feel slightly soft while warm, but it will be crunchy when fully cooled, about 10 minutes. Serve warm or store in an airtight container for up to 3 days for best freshness.

PER SERVING:

CALORIES: 245 | FAT: 12g | SODIUM: 654mg | CARBOHYDRATES: 29g | FIBER: 1g | SUGAR: 2g | PROTEIN: 4g

Spinach Artichoke Dip

This rich dip is always a crowd favorite. It's filled with vegetables and is very creamy, making it perfect for pairing with a crunchy tortilla chip or warm toasted piece of bread. If you like a browned top, transfer this dip to an oven-safe baking dish and broil the top on high 3 minutes until it's golden brown.

Hands-On Time: 5 minutes
Cook Time: 7 minutes

Serves 12

1 cup chicken broth
2 (10-ounce) packages frozen spinach, thawed and drained
1 cup sour cream
2 cup mayonnaise
2 teaspoons garlic powder
1 teaspoon salt
1 (7-ounce) can artichokes, drained and chopped
16 ounces cream cheese, cubed
3 cups mozzarella cheese
½ cup grated Parmesan cheese

1 Pour broth into an Instant Pot®. Add spinach, sour cream, mayonnaise, garlic powder, salt, and artichokes. Place cream cheese on top.

2 Place the lid on the Instant Pot® and click into place to close. Press the Pressure Cook button and adjust the timer to 7 minutes. When the timer beeps, quick-release the pressure until float valve drops. Unlock lid.

3 Stir in mozzarella and Parmesan until well combined. Serve warm.

PER SERVING:

CALORIES: 518 | FAT: 46g | SODIUM: 945mg | CARBOHYDRATES: 8g | FIBER: 2g | SUGAR: 3g | PROTEIN: 11g

Cajun Boiled Peanuts

Boiled peanuts are a staple snack in the southern United States, and thanks to your Instant Pot®, you can prepare them in a fraction of the time of the traditional method. The Cajun seasoning in this recipe elevates the flavor, making this irresistible snack even more enticing.

Hands-On Time: 5 minutes
Cook Time: 1 hour

Serves 5

5 cups green peanuts in shells
6 cups water
1 tablespoon Cajun seasoning
1 teaspoon salt
¼ cup pickled jalapeño slices

GREEN PEANUTS

Green peanuts, which have had no moisture removed after being harvested, are often used to make boiled peanuts. Raw peanuts, however, are dried, allowing for longer storage. They will work for this recipe, too, but for best results you should soak them in water overnight prior to cooking to ensure the right texture.

1 Place peanuts in an Instant Pot® and pour in water.

2 Sprinkle Cajun seasoning, salt, and jalapeños on top of peanuts. Place the lid on the Instant Pot® and click into place to close.

3 Press the Pressure Cook button and adjust the timer to 1 hour. When the timer beeps, allow a full natural release of pressure, about 20 minutes, until float valve drops. Unlock lid. Serve warm. Store leftovers in an airtight container in the refrigerator for up to 5 days.

PER SERVING:

CALORIES: 200 | FAT: 13g | SODIUM: 487mg | CARBOHYDRATES: 13g | FIBER: 6g | SUGAR: 2g | PROTEIN: 9g

Grape Jelly Meatballs

These crowd-pleasing meatballs are the perfect balance of savory and sweet, and they're easy to make. Grape jelly is the star ingredient behind the delectable sauce, but you can experiment with other equally delicious variations such as jellied cranberry sauce or orange marmalade. For a festive presentation, serve the meatballs on toothpicks.

Hands-On Time: 5 minutes
Cook Time: 14 minutes

Serves 5

1 pound frozen cooked
   meatballs
½ cup water
½ cup grape jelly
½ cup barbecue sauce
3 tablespoons chili sauce

1 Place all ingredients in an Instant Pot® and stir to combine.

2 Place the lid on the Instant Pot® and click into place to close. Press the Pressure Cook button and adjust the timer to 7 minutes. When the timer beeps, quick-release the pressure until float valve drops. Unlock lid.

3 Stir meatballs to coat them in sauce. They should have an internal temperature of at least 160°F. Press the Cancel button, then the Sauté button. Stirring frequently, sauté meatballs and sauce 7 minutes. Sauce will thicken, creating a thick dark brown coating on meatballs. Little sauce will be left in the pot when done. Serve warm.

PER SERVING:

CALORIES: 399 | FAT: 18g | SODIUM: 910mg | CARBOHYDRATES: 41g | FIBER: 3g | SUGAR: 28g | PROTEIN: 14g

Barbecue Mini Smoked Sausages

Cooking the sausages in pineapple juice adds a fruity flavor to this otherwise savory appetizer. And the extra sweetness makes the sauce thick and sticky.

Hands-On Time: 5 minutes
Cook Time: 12 minutes

Serves 12

1 pound mini smoked sausages, such as Lit'l Smokies
1 cup pineapple juice
1 cup barbecue sauce

1 Place all ingredients in an Instant Pot® and stir to combine. Place the lid on the Instant Pot® and click into place to close.

2 Press the Pressure Cook button and adjust the timer to 7 minutes. When the timer beeps, quick-release the pressure until float valve drops. Unlock lid.

3 Press the Cancel button, then the Sauté button. Allow sauce to reduce 5 minutes, stirring frequently. When done, sauce should be able to coat the back of a spoon. Serve warm.

PER SERVING:

CALORIES: 165 | **FAT:** 10g | **SODIUM:** 631mg | **CARBOHYDRATES:** 13g | **FIBER:** 0g | **SUGAR:** 11g | **PROTEIN:** 5g

Applesauce

You can play around with different tastes in this recipe by switching up the types of apples, and with different textures by blending the applesauce for a longer or shorter time.

Hands-On Time: 5 minutes
Cook Time: 8 minutes

Serves 10

2 pounds Gala apples, peeled, cored, and quartered
1 cup water
1 tablespoon lemon juice
¼ cup granulated sugar

1 Place apples in an Instant Pot®, then pour water and lemon juice into the pot. Sprinkle sugar over apples. Place the lid on the Instant Pot® and click into place to close.

2 Press the Pressure Cook button and adjust the timer to 8 minutes. When the timer beeps, quick-release the pressure until float valve drops. Unlock lid.

3 Use a potato masher to mash apples until mostly smooth. Serve warm or chilled.

PER SERVING:

CALORIES: 52 | **FAT:** 0g | **SODIUM:** 0mg | **CARBOHYDRATES:** 14g | **FIBER:** 1g | **SUGAR:** 12g | **PROTEIN:** 0g

Restaurant-Style Red Salsa

Sometimes all you need for an appetizer are crispy tortilla chips and a delicious bowl of salsa. This recipe is very easy to make at home. You can customize it with your favorite flavors, too, so if you prefer spicy salsa, add a chopped medium jalapeño.

Hands-On Time: 5 minutes
Cook Time: 8 minutes

Serves 12

3 pounds plum tomatoes, cored and seeded

1 medium white onion, peeled and chopped

2 medium green bell peppers, seeded and diced

3 medium cloves garlic, peeled and minced

2 teaspoons salt

¼ teaspoon granulated sugar

½ cup water

½ cup fresh lime juice

½ cup chopped fresh cilantro

1 Place tomatoes, onion, bell peppers, garlic, salt, sugar, water, and lime juice in an Instant Pot®. Place the lid on the Instant Pot® and click into place to close. Press the Pressure Cook button and adjust the timer to 3 minutes. When the timer beeps, quick-release the pressure until float valve drops. Unlock lid.

2 Press the Cancel button. The vegetables should be soft enough to mash easily. Use a potato masher to break down pieces of vegetables until only small chunks remain.

3 Press the Sauté button on the Instant Pot®. Allow salsa to reduce 5 minutes to thicken. Stir in cilantro, then chill 45 minutes before serving.

PER SERVING:

CALORIES: 29 | FAT: 0g | SODIUM: 394mg | CARBOHYDRATES: 7g | FIBER: 2g | SUGAR: 4g | PROTEIN: 1g

Spicy Chicken Sliders

Party sliders are always a treat. They're great for game day, but they're also great for snacks because they're packed with protein. These juicy sliders are spicy and delicious. You might find yourself reaching for more than one!

Hands-On Time: 10 minutes
Cook Time: 5 minutes

Serves 8

1 pound ground chicken breast
¼ cup Italian-style bread crumbs
¼ cup chopped pickled jalapeños
¼ cup shredded pepper jack cheese
¼ medium red onion, peeled and diced
1 cup water
1 teaspoon salt
¼ teaspoon ground black pepper
4 (1-ounce) slices pepper jack cheese
8 slider buns
½ cup barbecue sauce

GROUND CHICKEN BREAST

In the last few years, ground chicken has become more popular at the grocery store. You may have even walked past it without noticing, but it's a light and delicious alternative to ground beef or turkey. It's sold most often in rectangular plastic containers, but you might also find it in a roll form. It's usually next to the fresh chicken.

1 In a large bowl, mix chicken, bread crumbs, jalapeños, shredded pepper jack, and onion until well combined. On a plate, separate mixture into eight even portions and form into patties, about 3" in diameter and ½" thick.

2 Pour water into an Instant Pot® and place a steamer basket in the pot, then place patties in basket. Sprinkle each side with salt and pepper. Place the lid on the Instant Pot® and click into place to close. Press the Pressure Cook button and adjust the timer to 5 minutes. When the timer beeps, quick-release the pressure until float valve drops. Unlock lid.

3 When patties are done, internal temperature should be at least 165°F. Place ½ slice pepper jack on top of each burger, then place each burger on the bottom of a slider bun. Add 1 tablespoon barbecue sauce on top of cheese and top with slider bun tops. Serve warm.

PER SERVING:

CALORIES: 295 | **FAT:** 12g | **SODIUM:** 857mg | **CARBOHYDRATES:** 29g | **FIBER:** 2g | **SUGAR:** 9g | **PROTEIN:** 19g

Mini Greek Turkey Meatballs

These small bites make excellent appetizers to serve on toothpicks, or delicious protein-filled snacks to enjoy alongside vegetables and hummus. Each bite is moist and packed with fresh flavor.

Hands-On Time: 10 minutes
Cook Time: 5 minutes

Serves 10

1 cup finely chopped spinach
½ cup crumbled feta cheese
½ medium red bell pepper, seeded and chopped
¼ medium red onion, peeled and chopped
¼ cup mayonnaise
½ cup Italian-style bread crumbs
1 teaspoon salt
¼ teaspoon ground black pepper
1 pound 93/7 ground turkey
1 cup water
¼ cup lemon juice
1 cup tzatziki sauce

1 Place spinach, feta, bell pepper, and onion in a food processor and pulse ten times until ingredients are broken down into small pieces. Add mayonnaise, bread crumbs, salt, and black pepper, then pulse five more times until well incorporated. Transfer mixture to a large bowl and mix with turkey until well combined.

2 Divide and roll mixture into thirty 1" balls. Pour water and lemon juice into an Instant Pot®, then place meatballs in the pot. Place the lid on the Instant Pot® and click into place to close. Press the Pressure Cook button and adjust the timer to 5 minutes.

3 When the timer beeps, let the pressure release naturally for 5 minutes, then quick-release any remaining pressure until float valve drops. Unlock lid. When done, meatballs should have an internal temperature of at least 165°F. Serve warm on toothpicks with tzatziki sauce.

PER SERVING:

CALORIES: 185 | FAT: 11g | SODIUM: 526mg | CARBOHYDRATES: 8g | FIBER: 1g | SUGAR: 3g | PROTEIN: 13g

Bacon and Cream Cheese–Stuffed Mushrooms

This soft, creamy appetizer is a dream for mushroom and bacon lovers! The easy-prep recipe is great to make for dinner parties or when you simply want a savory snack. For browned tops, after they're done pressure cooking, place the filled mushroom caps on a foil-lined baking sheet and broil in oven 3 minutes.

Hands-On Time: 10 minutes
Cook Time: 13 minutes

Serves 4

- 4 slices bacon, chopped
- 2 ounces cream cheese, softened
- ¼ cup grated Parmesan cheese
- ¼ cup Italian bread crumbs
- 12 baby bella mushrooms, stems removed
- ½ teaspoon salt
- ¼ teaspoon ground black pepper
- 1 tablespoon olive oil
- 1 cup water

1 Press the Sauté button on an Instant Pot® and allow to heat until the display reads "Hot." Place bacon in the pot and sauté until browned and crispy, about 5 minutes. Press the Cancel button. Spoon bacon into a large bowl, then drain grease and wipe pot completely clean before returning to the base.

2 In large bowl with bacon, add cream cheese, Parmesan, and bread crumbs, then stir until well combined. Spoon a heaping tablespoon of mixture into each mushroom cap and sprinkle with salt and pepper, then drizzle with olive oil. Pour water into an Instant Pot® and place a steamer basket in the pot, then place mushrooms in basket.

3 Place the lid on the Instant Pot® and click into place to close. Press the Pressure Cook button and adjust the timer to 8 minutes. When the timer beeps, quick-release the pressure until float valve drops. Unlock lid. Serve warm.

PER SERVING:

CALORIES: 171 | FAT: 13g | SODIUM: 651mg | CARBOHYDRATES: 4g | FIBER: 0g | SUGAR: 1g | PROTEIN: 8g

Barbecue Wings

This recipe is a game-day classic. Making wings in the Instant Pot® gives you super tender meat that's quickly infused with flavor. The skin will not crisp while being pressure cooked, but that's nothing a quick broil in the oven won't fix. It will take less time overall, and you'll still be able to enjoy that crispy, caramelized barbecue taste.

Hands-On Time: 5 minutes
Cook Time: 15 minutes

Serves 5

2 pounds chicken wings, drums and flats separated
2 teaspoons salt
½ teaspoon ground black pepper
¼ teaspoon garlic powder
¼ teaspoon paprika
⅛ teaspoon ground oregano
1 cup water
¾ cup barbecue sauce

1   In a large bowl, toss wings with salt, pepper, garlic powder, paprika, and oregano. Pour water into an Instant Pot® and place a steamer basket in the pot, then place wings in basket.

2   Place the lid on the Instant Pot® and click into place to close. Press the Pressure Cook button and adjust the timer to 10 minutes. When the timer beeps, quick-release the pressure until float valve drops. Unlock lid.

3   Line a baking sheet with aluminum foil. Transfer wings to a clean large bowl, add barbecue sauce, and toss to coat. Place wings on prepared sheet, then place on top rack of oven and broil 5 minutes to caramelize barbecue sauce. When done, wings will be dark brown and have an internal temperature of at least 165°F. Serve warm.

PER SERVING:

CALORIES: 420 | FAT: 22g | SODIUM: 1,503mg | CARBOHYDRATES: 18g | FIBER: 1g | SUGAR: 14g | PROTEIN: 33g

Popcorn

You might think the Instant Pot® is just for pressure cooking, but the Sauté function is your ticket to perfect, fluffy popcorn made in minutes. The kernels pop evenly, making each batch crunchy with little waste.

Hands-On Time: 5 minutes
Cook Time: 5 minutes

Serves 4

3 tablespoons refined coconut oil

½ cup yellow popcorn kernels

2 tablespoons salted butter, melted

½ teaspoon salt

COCONUT OIL

Refined coconut oil is a completely flavorless oil with a high smoke point, which makes it the perfect cooking oil for this recipe. If you don't mind coconut flavor, unrefined coconut oil will work too. If you cannot use coconut oil, ghee or vegetable oil are both suitable substitutes but will affect flavor.

1 Press the Sauté button on an Instant Pot® and adjust the temperature to "More." Pour oil into the pot. Once the display panel reads "Hot," add popcorn kernels.

2 Place a glass slow cooker lid on the pot to keep popped kernels from escaping. Holding the side handles of the Instant Pot®, gently move the pot back and forth on the counter to spread the kernels.

3 Once kernels begin to pop, continue gently moving the Instant Pot® back and forth to evenly distribute heat and keep kernels from burning. Once the popping slows and the Instant Pot® is mostly full of popcorn, about 5 minutes, turn off the heat and remove the inner pot, placing it on a surface to cool. Remove the lid once popping completely stops. Top popcorn with butter and salt to serve.

PER SERVING:

CALORIES: 210 | **FAT:** 14g | **SODIUM:** 336mg | **CARBOHYDRATES:** 19g | **FIBER:** 3g | **SUGAR:** 0g | **PROTEIN:** 3g

Buffalo Chicken Wings

These wings have a secret ingredient: dry ranch seasoning! Coating the wings with flavor before they're steamed allows the flavors to cook into the meat. These wings are finished in the oven to crisp the skin.

Hands-On Time: 5 minutes
Cook Time: 15 minutes

Serves 5

2 pounds chicken wings, drums and flats separated

1 (1-ounce) packet dry ranch seasoning

1 cup plus 2 tablespoons water, divided

1 cup hot sauce

3 tablespoons salted butter

1 tablespoon cornstarch

1 In a large bowl, toss wings in ranch seasoning until well coated. Pour 1 cup water into an Instant Pot® and place a steamer basket in the pot, then place wings in basket.

2 Place the lid on the Instant Pot® and click into place to close. Press the Pressure Cook button and adjust the timer to 10 minutes. When the timer beeps, quick-release the pressure until float valve drops. Unlock lid. When done, wings should have an internal temperature of at least 165°F. Remove wings from the basket and set aside. Pour out water.

3 Press the Cancel button, then the Sauté button. Add hot sauce and butter to the pot. In a small bowl, whisk remaining 2 tablespoons water and cornstarch until smooth, then whisk mixture into hot sauce mixture. Place wings in the pot and continue sautéing and tossing with tongs 5 minutes until wings are well coated and dark red. The sauce will thicken as it cooks. Line a large baking sheet with aluminum foil and place wings on prepared sheet. Place on top rack of oven and broil 5 minutes until sauce begins to brown at the edges. Serve warm.

PER SERVING:

CALORIES: 428 | FAT: 29g | SODIUM: 2,084mg | CARBOHYDRATES: 5g | FIBER: 0g | SUGAR: 0g | PROTEIN: 32g

6

Side Dishes

When you're planning an entrée, it's always important to consider what food will be enjoyed on the side of the main dish. Side dishes are an important way to round out a meal, making it more filling and ensuring you are getting your vegetables. Often side dishes can be even more exciting than the main course...and your Instant Pot® can help you get those irresistible sides cooked in no time! Cooking side dishes in the Instant Pot® is especially convenient when the main dish is taking up your oven and you want everything done at the same time. From creamy Macaroni and Cheese to Green Bean Casserole, this chapter's recipes are sure to help you level up your entrées.

Baked Potatoes 92

Petite Golden Potatoes 93

Macaroni and Cheese 94

Mashed Potatoes 96

Mustard Potato Salad 97

Corn Bread 98

Steamed Green Beans 99

Lemon Pepper Brussels Sprouts 101

Steamed Lemon Broccoli 102

Garlic Spread 103

Maple-Glazed Carrots 104

Corn on the Cob 104

Green Bean Casserole 105

Cinnamon Butternut Squash 106

Cranberry Sauce 108

Buttery Cabbage 108

Baked Potatoes

Who doesn't love a fluffy baked potato? They can take nearly an hour to bake in the oven, but these steamed potatoes are tender and ready for all your favorite toppings such as bacon, sour cream, and chives. If you're a fan of broccoli, you can even pour cheese sauce and steamed broccoli on top.

Hands-On Time: 5 minutes
Cook Time: 20 minutes

Serves 4

1 cup water
4 medium russet potatoes
1 tablespoon salted butter, melted
2 teaspoons coarse sea salt

GET CREATIVE!

Baked potatoes are great with the classic butter and sour cream. You can also get creative using leftovers and try a barbecue loaded potato. Add shredded barbecue meat, Cheddar, and crunchy fried onions. You could also add slices of cooked steak, chives, and bacon for a steakhouse–worthy dish.

1 Pour water into an Instant Pot® and place the trivet in the pot. Poke potatoes multiple times with a fork to create venting holes. Brush each potato with butter and sprinkle with salt.

2 Place potatoes on trivet in a single layer. Place the lid on the Instant Pot® and click into place to close. Press the Pressure Cook button and adjust the timer to 20 minutes.

3 When the timer beeps, quick-release the pressure until float valve drops. Unlock lid. When done, potatoes should be easily pierced with a fork. Carefully remove potatoes with tongs and let cool at least 10 minutes before serving.

PER SERVING:

CALORIES: 193 | FAT: 3g | SODIUM: 1,006mg | CARBOHYDRATES: 37g | FIBER: 4g | SUGAR: 2g | PROTEIN: 5g

Petite Golden Potatoes

This is the perfect side dish for just about any dinner. Golden potatoes are often less than 1" long and tend to have a creamier taste compared to russet potatoes. This recipe steams them, then gives them a crispy, seasoned coating.

Hands-On Time: 5 minutes
Cook Time: 13 minutes

Serves 4

1 pound petite Yukon Gold
  potatoes
1 cup water
2 tablespoons olive oil
½ teaspoon salt
¼ teaspoon ground black
  pepper

1 Place potatoes in a steamer basket. Pour water into an Instant Pot® and place basket in the pot.

2 Place the lid on the Instant Pot® and click into place to close. Press the Pressure Cook button and adjust the timer to 9 minutes. When the timer beeps, quick-release the pressure until float valve drops. Unlock lid.

3 Press the Cancel button. Remove basket and potatoes and pour out water. Wipe the pot dry, then return to the base. Press the Sauté button on the Instant Pot® and allow to heat until the display reads "Hot." Drizzle olive oil over potatoes and sprinkle with salt and pepper. Sauté potatoes until the skins are golden brown, about 4 minutes. Serve warm.

PER SERVING:

CALORIES: 166 | **FAT:** 7g | **SODIUM:** 298mg | **CARBOHYDRATES:** 24g | **FIBER:** 2g | **SUGAR:** 2g | **PROTEIN:** 2g

Macaroni and Cheese

One you make this Macaroni and Cheese recipe, it will become your favorite! It's so easy that you won't even want to bother with a boxed mix again. This version uses four cheeses to create the perfect gooey, tangy, and creamy sauce. Each spoonful overflows with melted cheese. Feel free to add a dash of hot sauce or sprinkle the top with crispy cooked pieces of bacon.

Hands-On Time: 10 minutes
Cook Time: 5 minutes

Serves 6

2 cups chicken broth
2 cups dry elbow macaroni
½ teaspoon salt
¼ teaspoon ground black pepper
2 tablespoons salted butter
¼ cup whole milk
1 cup shredded sharp Cheddar cheese
1 cup shredded white Cheddar cheese
½ cup shredded mozzarella cheese
¼ cup grated Parmesan cheese

1 Pour broth into an Instant Pot®, then add macaroni, salt, pepper, and butter. Use a wooden spoon to stir. Place the lid on the Instant Pot® and click into place to close.

2 Press the Pressure Cook button and adjust the timer to 5 minutes. When the timer beeps, quick-release the pressure until float valve drops. Unlock lid.

3 Add remaining ingredients, stirring until cheese is melted and fully incorporated. Serve warm.

PER SERVING:

CALORIES: 366 | FAT: 17g | SODIUM: 904mg | CARBOHYDRATES: 29g | FIBER: 1g | SUGAR: 2g | PROTEIN: 17g

Mashed Potatoes

The key to good mashed potatoes is to not overmix them. Hand mixers are tempting but can disturb the starch and cause gummy potatoes. These potatoes come out fluffy and delicious. The dry ranch seasoning is a quick way to add lots of flavor to this dish, but if you aren't a fan of ranch flavor, feel free to omit and add a seasoning blend you prefer.

Hands-On Time: 5 minutes
Cook Time: 10 minutes

Serves 4

1 cup water
3 large russet potatoes, peeled and halved lengthwise
3 tablespoons salted butter
¼ cup sour cream
¼ cup whole milk
2 tablespoons dry ranch seasoning
½ teaspoon salt
¼ teaspoon ground black pepper

GUMMY POTATOES

Sometimes, despite our best efforts, we might accidentally overmix the potatoes and make them gummy, add too much butter, or just generally dislike the texture. If your potatoes seem too watery or gummy, add 1 tablespoon dry potato flakes at a time until they're fluffy.

1 Pour water into an Instant Pot® and place the trivet in the pot, then place potato halves on trivet. Place the lid on the Instant Pot® and click into place to close. Press the Pressure Cook button and adjust the timer to 10 minutes. When the timer beeps, quick-release the pressure until float valve drops. Unlock lid.

2 Carefully remove potato halves and set aside in a medium bowl. Remove trivet and pour out water. Return potatoes to the Instant Pot® and use a masher to break into pieces.

3 Add remaining ingredients to the Instant Pot®. Continue mashing 2 minutes until potatoes are fluffy and all ingredients are well incorporated. Serve warm.

PER SERVING:

CALORIES: 236 | **FAT:** 11g | **SODIUM:** 782mg | **CARBOHYDRATES:** 29g | **FIBER:** 2g | **SUGAR:** 3g | **PROTEIN:** 3g

Mustard Potato Salad

This recipe will make your summer barbecues even easier. Mustard adds a tasty tang to this classic dish, and the seasoned salt adds a lot of flavor with just one ingredient. Seasoned salt, such as Lawry's Seasoned Salt, is a great addition to any spice cabinet; it's a mixture of salt, garlic powder, onion powder, and often paprika for color.

Hands-On Time: 10 minutes
Cook Time: 6 minutes

Serves 10

1 cup water
6 medium russet potatoes, peeled and chopped into 1" cubes
2 large eggs
1 teaspoon seasoned salt
¼ teaspoon ground black pepper
1½ cups mayonnaise
2 teaspoons yellow mustard
2 medium stalks celery, trimmed and chopped
¼ teaspoon celery salt
¼ cup sweet relish

1   Pour water into an Instant Pot® and place a steamer basket in the pot, then place potatoes in basket and place whole eggs on top of potatoes. Sprinkle potatoes with seasoned salt and pepper. Place the lid on the Instant Pot® and click into place to close. Press the Pressure Cook button and adjust the timer to 6 minutes. When the timer beeps, quick-release the pressure until float valve drops. Unlock lid.

2   Carefully remove eggs (they will be hot). Place them in a small bowl of ice water 3 minutes, then peel and finely chop. Place potatoes and eggs in a large bowl.

3   In a medium bowl, mix together mayonnaise, mustard, celery, celery salt, and relish until well combined. Pour mixture over potatoes and fold until all ingredients are well combined. Cover and chill at least 2 hours before serving.

PER SERVING:

CALORIES: 335 | FAT: 25g | SODIUM: 476mg | CARBOHYDRATES: 23g | FIBER: 2g | SUGAR: 4g | PROTEIN: 4g

Corn Bread

If you're enjoying a hot bowl of chili, a side of corn bread is a must. This version is sweet and textured—firm and fluffy—but since it is steamed, it won't be crunchy on top like it is when you bake it in the oven. Feel free to add sliced jalapeños and ¼ cup Cheddar cheese before baking.

Hands-On Time: 10 minutes
Cook Time: 55 minutes

Serves 6

1 cup buttermilk
1 large egg
¼ cup granulated sugar
¼ cup light brown sugar, packed
6 tablespoons salted butter, melted
1 cup all-purpose flour
1 teaspoon salt
1 cup cornmeal
1 tablespoon baking powder
1 cup water

1 In a medium bowl, whisk together buttermilk, egg, granulated sugar, brown sugar, and butter until well combined. In a large bowl, whisk together flour, salt, cornmeal, and baking powder until well combined. Pour wet ingredients into dry ingredients and stir until well combined.

2 Spray a 6" round baking pan with nonstick cooking spray. Pour batter into prepared pan and cover pan tightly with aluminum foil. Pour water into an Instant Pot® and place the trivet in the pot, then place pan on trivet.

3 Place the lid on the Instant Pot® and click into place to close. Press the Pressure Cook button and adjust the timer to 55 minutes. When the timer beeps, let the pressure release naturally for 10 minutes. Unlock lid. When done, corn bread should be firm to the touch and a toothpick inserted into the center should come out clean. Serve warm.

PER SERVING:

CALORIES: 356 | **FAT:** 13g | **SODIUM:** 786mg | **CARBOHYDRATES:** 52g | **FIBER:** 2g | **SUGAR:** 19g | **PROTEIN:** 6g

Steamed Green Beans

Frozen steamer bags can be tempting, and while they are a great option, don't overlook the flavor that fresh green beans can offer. They prep quickly, so you can enjoy delicious tender-crisp steamed fresh vegetables in no time. If you have access to local fresh green beans, the summer is one of the best times to buy because they're in season and have a yummy fresh-cut-from-the-garden taste that won't be lost in steaming.

Hands-On Time: 5 minutes

Cook Time: 1 minute

Serves 4

1 cup water

1 pound fresh green beans, ends trimmed

2 tablespoons salted butter, melted

½ teaspoon salt

¼ teaspoon ground black pepper

1 Pour water into an Instant Pot® and place a steamer basket in the pot, then place green beans in basket.

2 Place the lid on the Instant Pot® and click into place to close. Press the Pressure Cook button and adjust the timer to 1 minute. When the timer beeps, quick-release the pressure until float valve drops. Unlock lid.

3 Carefully remove green beans and place in a large bowl. Pour butter over green beans and toss to coat, then sprinkle with salt and pepper. Serve warm.

PER SERVING:

CALORIES: 81 | FAT: 6g | SODIUM: 341mg | CARBOHYDRATES: 7g | FIBER: 3g | SUGAR: 3g | PROTEIN: 2g

Lemon Pepper Brussels Sprouts

Steaming vegetables is a great cooking method because it allows more nutrients to be retained and the bright flavor to shine. This recipe is perfect to pair with chicken for a light and nutritious meal. You may have had Brussels sprouts before that were excessively mushy and fell apart, but these are just tender enough for a fork to go through. Less cooking keeps them fresh-tasting and delicious.

Hands-On Time: 5 minutes

Cook Time: 3 minutes

Serves 4

1 pound Brussels sprouts, halved

2 tablespoons salted butter

½ teaspoon salt

¼ teaspoon ground black pepper

1½ tablespoons lemon juice

1½ teaspoons grated lemon zest

1 cup chicken broth

1 Place Brussels sprouts, butter, salt, pepper, lemon juice, and lemon zest in an ungreased 6" round baking pan. Cover pan tightly with aluminum foil.

2 Pour broth into an Instant Pot® and place the trivet in the pot, then place pan on trivet. Place the lid on the Instant Pot® and click into place to close. Press the Pressure Cook button and adjust the timer to 3 minutes.

3 When the timer beeps, quick-release the pressure until float valve drops. Unlock lid. Brussels sprouts will be crisp and tender. Serve warm.

PER SERVING:

CALORIES: 88 | FAT: 6g | SODIUM: 356mg | CARBOHYDRATES: 8g | FIBER: 3g | SUGAR: 2g | PROTEIN: 3g

Steamed Lemon Broccoli

Broccoli is full of nutrients, making it an excellent choice for side dishes. Fresh citrus can brighten up the entire dish and make it feel like new, even if you feel like you eat broccoli all of the time. If you're unable to use fresh lemon, try adding ½ teaspoon dry lemon pepper seasoning for a burst of flavor.

Hands-On Time: 5 minutes
Cook Time: 2 minutes

Serves 4

1 cup water
2 cups fresh broccoli florets
1 tablespoon olive oil
½ teaspoon salt
¼ teaspoon ground black pepper
2 tablespoons lemon zest

LOAD IT UP!

This recipe is a great base for loaded broccoli. This idea is a delicious low-carb ode to the stuffed baked potato. You simply top the steamed broccoli with your choice of shredded Cheddar cheese, sour cream, and cooked bacon pieces.

1 Pour water into an Instant Pot® and place a steamer basket in the pot, then place broccoli in basket. Place the lid on the Instant Pot® and click into place to close.

2 Press the Pressure Cook button and adjust the timer to 2 minutes. When the timer beeps, quick-release the pressure until float valve drops. Unlock lid. Carefully remove basket and transfer broccoli to a large bowl.

3 Pour olive oil over broccoli, then sprinkle with salt, pepper, and lemon zest. Toss to combine. Serve warm.

PER SERVING:

CALORIES: 46 | **FAT**: 3g | **SODIUM**: 305mg | **CARBOHYDRATES**: 4g | **FIBER**: 2g | **SUGAR**: 1g | **PROTEIN**: 1g

Garlic Spread

This recipe is easy and versatile. You can spread it on a slice of bread, use it as a sauce on pizza, or use a spoonful in recipes to add some extra flavor. To double this recipe, simply wrap two heads of garlic in two separate aluminum foil packets and double the olive oil. The cook time and water amount remain the same.

Hands-On Time: 5 minutes
Cook Time: 10 minutes

Serves 8

1 head garlic, top removed
¼ cup olive oil, divided
1 cup water

FREEZING GARLIC SPREAD

The best way to freeze garlic spread is using a silicone candy mold. You can find a mold where each well holds 1 teaspoon of a filling. Fill the mold; once the garlic paste is frozen, simply pop out the frozen pieces and transfer them to a freezer-safe storage bag. You'll know exactly how much garlic paste you have in each piece, and you won't even need to defrost if you're adding it to an Instant Pot® meal; just add it straight to the pot.

1   Place garlic on a 6" × 6" square of aluminum foil, then drizzle with 1 tablespoon olive oil. Wrap the foil tightly around garlic. Pour water into an Instant Pot® and place the trivet in the pot, then place wrapped garlic on trivet.

2   Place the lid on the Instant Pot® and click into place to close. Press the Pressure Cook button and adjust the timer to 10 minutes. When the timer beeps, quick-release the pressure until float valve drops. Unlock lid. Carefully remove wrapped garlic with tongs and let cool on the counter 10 minutes before unwrapping.

3   Squeeze softened garlic cloves into a medium bowl and use a fork to smash into a thick paste. Whisk in remaining olive oil until well incorporated. Store in an airtight container in the refrigerator for up to 2 weeks.

PER SERVING:

CALORIES: 66 | **FAT**: 7g | **SODIUM**: 0mg | **CARBOHYDRATES**: 1g | **FIBER**: 0g | **SUGAR**: 0g | **PROTEIN**: 0g

Maple-Glazed Carrots

This side dish is perfect alongside chicken, a roast, or even Thanksgiving dinner. Easily double this recipe by doubling everything except the water and keeping the cook time the same.

Hands-On Time: 5 minutes
Cook Time: 2 minutes

Serves 4

1 pound baby carrots
2 tablespoons salted butter, cubed
¼ teaspoon salt
½ tablespoon ground cinnamon
¼ cup pure maple syrup
1 cup water

1 Place carrots, butter, salt, cinnamon, and maple syrup in a 6" round baking pan. Pour water into an Instant Pot® and place the trivet in the pot, then place pan on trivet.

2 Place the lid on the Instant Pot® and click into place to close. Press the Pressure Cook button and adjust the timer to 2 minutes.

3 When the timer beeps, quick-release the pressure until float valve drops. Unlock lid. When done, carrots will be tender. Gently toss carrots to coat in sauce. Serve warm.

PER SERVING:

CALORIES: 150 | **FAT:** 6g | **SODIUM:** 271mg | **CARBOHYDRATES:** 25g | **FIBER:** 4g | **SUGAR:** 17g | **PROTEIN:** 1g

Corn on the Cob

This easy recipe works well for both big and small batches. Feel free to double a batch by simply doubling the corn, butter, and salt and stacking the corn inside the pot.

Hands-On Time: 5 minutes
Cook Time: 2 minutes

Serves 4

1 cup water
4 medium ears corn, husks and silk removed
2 tablespoons salted butter, melted
½ teaspoon salt

1 Pour water into an Instant Pot® and place a steamer basket in the pot, then place corn in basket. Place the lid on the Instant Pot® and click into place to close.

2 Press the Pressure Cook button and adjust the timer to 2 minutes. When the timer beeps, quick-release the pressure until float valve drops. Unlock lid.

3 Use tongs to transfer corn to a serving platter. Pour butter over cobs and sprinkle with salt. Serve warm.

PER SERVING:

CALORIES: 138 | **FAT:** 7g | **SODIUM:** 351mg | **CARBOHYDRATES:** 19g | **FIBER:** 2g | **SUGAR:** 6g | **PROTEIN:** 3g

Green Bean Casserole

This holiday classic cooks quicker than ever in the Instant Pot®. If your main course is taking a while in the oven, you can whip up this side in a few minutes and have it ready to go in no time. If you enjoy a crispy top, you can even add it to a baking dish and simply broil the top just before serving.

Hands-On Time: 5 minutes
Cook Time: 3 minutes

Serves 6

4 (14.5-ounce) cans cut green beans, drained (reserve ½ cup liquid)
1 (10.5-ounce) can cream of mushroom soup
½ teaspoon salt
¼ teaspoon ground black pepper
1 tablespoon cornstarch
¼ cup heavy cream
1 cup crispy fried onions

1 Pour reserved green bean liquid into an Instant Pot®, then add green beans, soup, salt, and pepper. Stir to combine. Place the lid on the Instant Pot® and click into place to close.

2 Press the Pressure Cook button and adjust the timer to 3 minutes. When the timer beeps, quick-release the pressure until float valve drops. Unlock lid.

3 Press the Cancel button, then the Sauté button. Whisk cornstarch and cream in a small bowl until well combined. Stir mixture into the pot and allow mixture to thicken 5 minutes, stirring frequently. Top with onions. Serve warm.

PER SERVING:

CALORIES: 113 | **FAT**: 7g | **SODIUM**: 968mg | **CARBOHYDRATES**: 12g | **FIBER**: 3g | **SUGAR**: 2g | **PROTEIN**: 3g

Cinnamon Butternut Squash

This sweet, spiced dish has all the feeling of a dessert, but you'll feel good knowing it's a nutritious vegetable. It has a soft, tender texture, and it has iron as well as vitamins A and C.

Hands-On Time: 10 minutes
Cook Time: 3 minutes

Serves 4

- 1 (2-pound) butternut squash, peeled, seeded, and diced into 1" cubes
- 2 tablespoons salted butter, melted
- 1 tablespoon light brown sugar, packed
- 1 tablespoon pure maple syrup
- ½ teaspoon ground cinnamon
- ¼ teaspoon salt
- 1 cup water

1 Spray a 6" round baking pan with nonstick cooking spray. Place squash in prepared pan. Pour butter over squash, then sprinkle with brown sugar, maple syrup, cinnamon, and salt. Cover pan tightly with aluminum foil.

2 Pour water into an Instant Pot® and place the trivet in the pot, then place pan on trivet. Place the lid on the Instant Pot® and click into place to close. Press the Pressure Cook button and adjust the timer to 3 minutes.

3 When the timer beeps, let the pressure release naturally for 3 minutes, then quick-release any remaining pressure until float valve drops. Unlock lid. Gently toss to coat squash in liquid before serving.

PER SERVING:

CALORIES: 139 | FAT: 5g | SODIUM: 198mg | CARBOHYDRATES: 23g | FIBER: 5g | SUGAR: 9g | PROTEIN: 1g

Cranberry Sauce

This side is great for the holidays and goes perfectly with roasted turkey and stuffing.

Hands-On Time: 5 minutes
Cook Time: 1 minute

Serves 8

12 ounces cranberries, rinsed and drained
1½ tablespoons grated orange zest
¼ cup orange juice
¾ cup water
½ cup granulated sugar

1 Place cranberries, orange zest and juice, and water in an Instant Pot®. Place the lid on the Instant Pot® and click into place to close. Press the Pressure Cook button and adjust the timer to 1 minute.

2 When the timer beeps, quick-release the pressure until float valve drops. Press the Cancel button. Unlock lid.

3 Use a spoon to break down cranberries, then stir in sugar. The mixture will thicken as it cools. Refrigerate 1 hour for chilled sauce.

PER SERVING:

CALORIES: 70 | FAT: 0g | SODIUM: 0mg | CARBOHYDRATES: 18g | FIBER: 2g | SUGAR: 15g | PROTEIN: 0g

Buttery Cabbage

Cabbage is loaded with nutrients but is often overlooked when it comes to side dishes.

Hands-On Time: 5 minutes
Cook Time: 5 minutes

Serves 4

1 medium head white cabbage, cored and sliced into ½"-thick strips
2 tablespoons salted butter, sliced
½ teaspoon salt
¼ teaspoon ground black pepper
1 cup water

1 Place cabbage in a 6" round baking pan. Place butter slices on top of cabbage and sprinkle with salt and pepper. Cover pan tightly with aluminum foil.

2 Pour water into an Instant Pot® and place the trivet in the pot, then place pan on trivet. Place the lid on the Instant Pot® and click into place to close.

3 Press the Pressure Cook button and adjust the timer to 5 minutes. When the timer beeps, quick-release the pressure until float valve drops. Unlock lid. Stir well. Serve warm.

PER SERVING:

CALORIES: 107 | FAT: 5g | SODIUM: 376mg | CARBOHYDRATES: 13g | FIBER: 6g | SUGAR: 7g | PROTEIN: 3g

Chicken Main Dishes

Chicken is the most popular meat in the world. It's high in protein, inexpensive, and absolutely delicious. You may be used to buying chicken and not really knowing what to do with it, falling into an uninspiring routine that leaves your family asking, "Chicken again!?"

Well, you won't have to worry about those groans after preparing the quick and easy recipes from this chapter. Refresh your chicken routine with your new favorites such as Jerk Chicken Thighs and Spicy Chicken Burgers!

Lemon Herb Whole Chicken 110

Shredded Chicken 111

Chicken Fajitas 113

Chicken and Mashed Potato Bowl 114

Creamy Ranch Chicken 115

Jerk Chicken Thighs 116

Lemon Garlic Chicken Thighs 117

Chicken Broccoli Alfredo 118

Italian Herb Chicken Drumsticks 120

Barbecue Chicken Drumsticks 121

Spicy Chicken Burgers 122

Pesto Chicken 123

Butter Chicken 125

Creamy Mushroom Smothered Chicken 126

Teriyaki Chicken 127

Cheesy Chicken and Rice 128

Avocado Lime Chicken Salad 129

Hawaiian Chicken 130

Italian Chicken Pasta 132

Lemon Herb Whole Chicken

Since chicken weight can vary greatly, be sure to find one that fits into your Instant Pot® and adjust the cook time accordingly. A general rule of thumb is 6 minutes per pound of chicken, then a standard 15-minute natural release followed by a quick release of pressure.

Hands-On Time: 10 minutes
Cook Time: 35 minutes

Serves 6

1 (5-pound) whole chicken
½ medium white onion, peeled
1 large carrot, cut in half
½ medium lemon
2 teaspoons salt
2 teaspoons Italian seasoning
½ teaspoon paprika
½ teaspoon garlic powder
½ teaspoon dried thyme
½ teaspoon dried rosemary
½ teaspoon ground black pepper
1 cup chicken broth

CHICKEN GRAVY

To make gravy, use a fine-mesh strainer to strain drippings from the Instant Pot®, then return only the broth to the pot. Press the Sauté button. Whisk together 3 tablespoons heavy whipping cream and 2 tablespoons cornstarch until smooth, then whisk mixture into the chicken broth until smooth. Pour in 2 teaspoons lemon juice and add ¼ teaspoon ground black pepper. Continue whisking while gravy thickens, about 5 minutes, then serve warm over the chicken.

1 Empty chicken cavity and stuff with onion, carrot, and lemon. Sprinkle both sides of chicken with salt, Italian seasoning, paprika, garlic powder, thyme, rosemary, and pepper.

2 Pour broth into an Instant Pot® and place the trivet in the pot, then place chicken on trivet. Place the lid on the Instant Pot® and click into place to close. Press the Pressure Cook button and adjust the timer to 35 minutes. When the timer beeps, let the pressure release naturally for 15 minutes, then quick-release any remaining pressure until float valve drops. Unlock lid.

3 Remove chicken and check to ensure internal temperature in various parts is at least 165°F. Discard vegetables, then let it rest 10 minutes before slicing. Serve warm.

PER SERVING:

CALORIES: 424 | **FAT:** 25g | **SODIUM:** 883mg | **CARBOHYDRATES:** 1g | **FIBER:** 0g | **SUGAR:** 0g | **PROTEIN:** 40g

Shredded Chicken

This easy recipe is the perfect base for meal prep. Whether you need a big batch for tacos or just a little to add to soup, this recipe couldn't be easier. This recipe calls for fresh chicken breasts, but if you're cooking from frozen, just add 5 minutes to the cook time for a total of 25.

Hands-On Time: 5 minutes
Cook Time: 20 minutes

Serves 4

1 cup chicken broth
1 pound boneless, skinless chicken breasts
1 teaspoon salt
1 teaspoon Italian seasoning
½ teaspoon garlic powder
¼ teaspoon onion powder
¼ teaspoon ground black pepper

SEASONING

This recipe includes a basic seasoning to give the chicken enough flavor to work great in a dip or casserole. Feel free to swap the seasonings for a packet of taco seasoning, ranch seasoning, or whatever best complements the dish you plan to use the chicken with.

1   Pour broth into an Instant Pot®. Place chicken in the pot and sprinkle with salt, Italian seasoning, garlic powder, onion powder, and pepper.

2   Place the lid on the Instant Pot® and click into place to close. Press the Pressure Cook button and adjust the timer to 20 minutes. When the timer beeps, quick-release the pressure until float valve drops. Unlock lid. When done, chicken should have an internal temperature of at least 165°F and shred easily.

3   Pour out broth from the Instant Pot® and use two forks or an electric hand mixer to shred chicken. Serve warm.

PER SERVING:

CALORIES: 121 | **FAT:** 3g | **SODIUM:** 744mg | **CARBOHYDRATES:** 1g | **FIBER:** 0g | **SUGAR:** 0g | **PROTEIN:** 23g

Chicken Fajitas

Fajitas are an excellent meal that's high in protein and filled with vegetables. It's easy to make a quick batch. By searing the chicken, you get nice browned pieces, and a short pressure cook time provides perfectly tender-crisp vegetables.

Hands-On Time: 10 minutes
Cook Time: 13 minutes

Serves 4

- 2 tablespoons olive oil
- 1 pound boneless, skinless chicken breasts, sliced into ¼"-thick strips
- 1 (1-ounce) packet fajita seasoning
- ½ cup lime juice
- ½ cup chicken broth
- 2 medium green bell peppers, seeded and cut into ½"-thick slices
- 1 medium red bell pepper, seeded and sliced into ½"-thick slices
- 1 medium yellow onion, peeled and sliced into ¼"-thick slices
- 2 teaspoons cornstarch
- 8 (6") flour tortillas, warmed
- 1 medium lime, cut into wedges

1 Press the Sauté button on an Instant Pot® and allow to heat until the display reads "Hot." Add olive oil, chicken, and fajita seasoning to the pot. Sauté until chicken is fully cooked, about 7 minutes. The internal temperature should be at least 165°F.

2 Press the Cancel button. Pour lime juice and broth into the pot and use a wooden spoon to scrape any browned bits from the bottom. Add bell peppers and onion to the pot and stir to combine. Place the lid on the Instant Pot® and click into place to close. Press the Pressure Cook button and adjust the timer to 1 minute. When the timer beeps, quick-release the pressure until float valve drops. Unlock lid.

3 Press the Cancel button. Scoop ¼ cup liquid from the pot into a medium bowl and whisk with cornstarch until smooth. Press the Sauté button on the Instant Pot® and stir in cornstarch mixture. Continue to sauté 5 minutes until mixture thickens. Spoon into warmed tortillas and serve with lime wedges.

PER SERVING:

CALORIES: 426 | FAT: 13g | SODIUM: 1,127mg | CARBOHYDRATES: 47g | FIBER: 4g | SUGAR: 6g | PROTEIN: 29g

Chicken and Mashed Potato Bowl

This is a one-pot dinner of comfort food at its finest. It's perfect for saving time and a mess in the kitchen. The chicken cooks in the bottom of the Instant Pot®, making a delicious zesty gravy while the potatoes steam above. The result is a delicious gravy-filled bowl of chicken and mashed potatoes with a ton of flavor and only one pot to clean!

Hands-On Time: 10 minutes
Cook Time: 15 minutes

Serves 4

1 cup chicken broth
1 (10.5-ounce) can condensed cream of chicken soup
1 (1-ounce) packet brown gravy mix
4 (4-ounce) boneless, skinless chicken breasts
1 pound petite yellow potatoes, halved
3 tablespoons dry ranch seasoning
¾ teaspoon salt
¼ teaspoon ground black pepper
1 teaspoon dried parsley
2 tablespoons salted butter, thinly sliced
2 tablespoons sour cream

ADD VEGETABLES!
Feel free to add your favorite vegetables to this meal. Corn, green beans, or broccoli can be great options to enjoy on the side, or layered right into this tasty dish.

1 Pour broth and soup into an Instant Pot®. Whisk in gravy mix. Place chicken in the pot and spoon mixture over chicken.

2 Place potato halves on top of chicken. Sprinkle chicken and potatoes with ranch seasoning, salt, pepper, and parsley. Scatter butter slices on top. Place the lid on the Instant Pot® and click into place to close. Press the Pressure Cook button and adjust the timer to 15 minutes. When the timer beeps, quick-release the pressure until float valve drops. Unlock lid.

3 Carefully remove potatoes and set aside in a large bowl. When done, chicken should have an internal temperature of at least 165°F and shred easily. Shred with two forks and leave in the pot with the sauce. Add sour cream to bowl with potatoes and mash. Top with chicken and gravy. Serve warm.

PER SERVING:

CALORIES: 392 | FAT: 16g | SODIUM: 2,297mg | CARBOHYDRATES: 31g | FIBER: 6g | SUGAR: 2g | PROTEIN: 29g

Creamy Ranch Chicken

This comforting recipe is a delicious addition to any weeknight meal plan. The ranch seasoning doesn't make it taste like dressing but instead adds yummy herb and buttermilk flavors. This dish can be mixed in with pasta or simply enjoyed with a side of steamed broccoli. For extra crunch, try topping with fried onion pieces or chopped cooked bacon.

Hands-On Time: 5 minutes

Cook Time: 20 minutes

Serves 6

1 cup chicken broth

1 pound boneless, skinless chicken breasts

1 (1-ounce) packet dry ranch seasoning

2 tablespoons salted butter, cubed

8 ounces cream cheese

1 cup shredded sharp Cheddar cheese

1 Add broth and chicken to an Instant Pot®. Sprinkle with ranch seasoning. Place butter and cream cheese on top.

2 Place the lid on the Instant Pot® and click into place to close. Press the Pressure Cook button and adjust the timer to 20 minutes. When the timer beeps, quick-release the pressure until float valve drops. Unlock lid. When done, chicken should have an internal temperature of at least 165°F.

3 Using an electric hand mixer, shred chicken directly in the Instant Pot®, mixing all ingredients together until creamy. Fold in Cheddar until well combined. Serve warm.

PER SERVING:

CALORIES: 339 | FAT: 22g | SODIUM: 897mg | CARBOHYDRATES: 5g | FIBER: 0g | SUGAR: 1g | PROTEIN: 24g

Jerk Chicken Thighs

These Jamaican-inspired chicken thighs are full of spice and Caribbean flavor. For the most authentic taste, you'll want to season your chicken with a traditional jerk blend that uses Scotch bonnet peppers.

Hands-On Time: 10 minutes
Cook Time: 20 minutes

Serves 6

1½ pounds boneless, skinless chicken thighs
1 tablespoon olive oil
1 tablespoon jerk seasoning blend
½ medium white onion, peeled and sliced
½ cup pineapple juice
½ cup chicken broth

JERK SEASONING

Walkerswood is a favorite brand of seasoning that can be found at most grocery stores. It's a thick paste and coats the chicken really well compared to dry seasoning. It comes in mild and hot versions, but keep in mind that because of the ingredients, even the mild might taste a bit spicy to sensitive palates.

1 Place chicken thighs in a large bowl and drizzle with olive oil. Sprinkle with jerk seasoning and rub seasoning into chicken.

2 Place onion in an Instant Pot® and pour in pineapple juice and broth. Place the trivet in the pot, then put chicken thighs on trivet. Place the lid on the Instant Pot® and click into place to close.

3 Press the Pressure Cook button and adjust the timer to 20 minutes. When the timer beeps, quick-release the pressure until float valve drops. Unlock lid. When done, chicken should have an internal temperature of at least 165°F. Serve warm.

PER SERVING:

CALORIES: 168 | **FAT:** 8g | **SODIUM:** 137mg | **CARBOHYDRATES:** 0g | **FIBER:** 0g | **SUGAR:** 0g | **PROTEIN:** 21g

Lemon Garlic Chicken Thighs

Chicken thighs are full of flavor, easy to work with, and budget friendly! This quick dish requires mostly pantry ingredients, so it's a great last-minute meal idea. These are also great for meal prep. They reheat well in the air fryer for 5 minutes at 220°F until they're golden brown on the edges. Or warm for 10 minutes in a 350°F oven.

Hands-On Time: 5 minutes
Cook Time: 22 minutes

Serves 4

4 (4-ounce) boneless, skinless chicken thighs
1 tablespoon olive oil
½ teaspoon salt
½ teaspoon ground black pepper
½ teaspoon garlic powder
1 teaspoon Italian seasoning
1 large lemon, sliced
¼ cup lemon juice
1 cup chicken broth
1 tablespoon cornstarch
2 tablespoons water
¼ cup milk

1 Press the Sauté button on an Instant Pot® and allow to heat until the display reads "Hot." Place chicken thighs in the pot and then coat both sides with olive oil, salt, pepper, garlic powder, and Italian seasoning. Sear chicken on each side until golden brown, about 1 minute per side.

2 Press the Cancel button. Remove chicken and place 1 lemon slice on each thigh. Pour lemon juice and broth into the Instant Pot® and use a wooden spoon to scrape any browned bits from the bottom. Place the trivet in the pot, then place chicken thighs and lemon slices on trivet.

3 Place the lid on the Instant Pot® and click into place to close. Press the Pressure Cook button and adjust the timer to 15 minutes. When the timer beeps, quick-release the pressure until float valve drops. Unlock lid. When done, chicken should have an internal temperature of at least 165°F. Remove chicken and set aside. Press the Cancel button, then the Sauté button. In a small bowl, whisk cornstarch and water together until smooth, then whisk mixture into the pot with milk. Whisk until mixture thickens, about 5 minutes, then serve with chicken as a sauce. Serve warm.

PER SERVING:

CALORIES: 202 | FAT: 10g | SODIUM: 592mg | CARBOHYDRATES: 4g | FIBER: 0g | SUGAR: 1g | PROTEIN: 22g

Chicken Broccoli Alfredo

This classic dish comes together quickly for a dinner ready in less than 30 minutes, and it takes only a few ingredients to make your own sauce. This recipe uses already-cooked chicken, so feel free to grab a rotisserie chicken and shred away, or use the Shredded Chicken recipe in this chapter.

Hands-On Time: 10 minutes
Cook Time: 7 minutes

Serves 5

2 cups shredded cooked chicken
2 cups uncooked penne pasta
2½ cups chicken broth
1 cup frozen broccoli florets
3 tablespoons salted butter
1 teaspoon Italian seasoning
½ teaspoon salt
¼ teaspoon ground black pepper
⅔ cup whole milk
⅓ cup heavy whipping cream
½ cup grated Parmesan cheese

1 Place chicken, penne, broth, broccoli, butter, Italian seasoning, salt, and pepper in an Instant Pot®. Place the lid on the pot and click into place to close. Press the Pressure Cook button and adjust the timer to 5 minutes.

2 When the timer beeps, quick-release the pressure until float valve drops. Unlock lid. Pour in milk and cream, stirring quickly until well combined.

3 While the Instant Pot® is on Keep Warm mode, sprinkle in Parmesan and continue stirring until sauce begins to thicken and coat pasta, about 2 minutes. Serve warm.

PER SERVING:

CALORIES: 401 | FAT: 17g | SODIUM: 1,146mg | CARBOHYDRATES: 31g | FIBER: 2g | SUGAR: 4g | PROTEIN: 27g

Italian Herb Chicken Drumsticks

These drumsticks are fall-off-the-bone tender and packed with flavor. Drumsticks are a great budget dinner, but they're often overlooked as part of a regular dinner rotation. This dish pairs well with a side of Mashed Potatoes (see recipe in Chapter 6) or Creamy Lemon Orzo (see recipe in Chapter 4).

Hands-On Time: 5 minutes
Cook Time: 16 minutes 30 seconds

Serves 8

8 (4-ounce) chicken drumsticks, skin removed
2 tablespoons olive oil
1 teaspoon salt
¼ teaspoon ground black pepper
½ teaspoon garlic powder
2 teaspoons Italian seasoning
1 cup chicken broth
¼ cup grated Parmesan cheese
2 tablespoons chopped fresh parsley

1   Press the Sauté button on an Instant Pot® and allow to heat until the display reads "Hot." Place drumsticks in a large bowl. Drizzle olive oil over drumsticks and then sprinkle with salt, pepper, garlic powder, and Italian seasoning. Place drumsticks in the Instant Pot® and sear each side 45 seconds until golden brown.

2   Remove drumsticks with tongs and set aside on a large plate. The internal temperature should be at least 165°F. Press the Cancel button. Pour broth into the Instant Pot® and use a wooden spoon to scrape any browned bits from the bottom. Place a steamer basket in the pot, then place drumsticks in basket, using stackable baskets if needed. Place the lid on the Instant Pot® and click into place to close.

3   Press the Pressure Cook button and adjust the timer to 15 minutes. When the timer beeps, quick-release the pressure until float valve drops. Unlock lid. Sprinkle drumsticks with Parmesan and parsley. Serve warm.

PER SERVING:

CALORIES: 121 | FAT: 6g | SODIUM: 384mg | CARBOHYDRATES: 1g | FIBER: 0g | SUGAR: 0g | PROTEIN: 14g

Barbecue Chicken Drumsticks

Who doesn't love a delicious drumstick covered in sticky barbecue sauce? This dinner is a kid favorite, but so tasty that adults love it too. The Instant Pot® steams the chicken to perfection, and then the oven broiler gives them a delicious, caramelized coating.

Hands-On Time: 5 minutes
Cook Time: 21 minutes 30 seconds

Serves 8

8 (4-ounce) chicken drumsticks, skin removed
2 tablespoons olive oil
1 teaspoon salt
¼ teaspoon ground black pepper
½ teaspoon garlic powder
½ teaspoon paprika
¼ teaspoon onion powder
¼ teaspoon oregano
1¼ cups barbecue sauce, divided
1 cup chicken broth

1 Press the Sauté button on an Instant Pot® and allow to heat until the display reads "Hot." Place drumsticks in a large bowl. Drizzle olive oil over drumsticks, then sprinkle with salt, pepper, garlic powder, paprika, onion powder, and oregano. Place drumsticks in the pot and sear each side 45 seconds until golden brown. Press the Cancel button.

2 Pour 1 cup barbecue sauce and broth into the pot. Place the lid on the Instant Pot® and click into place to close. Press the Pressure Cook button and adjust the timer to 15 minutes. When the timer beeps, quick-release the pressure until float valve drops. Unlock lid. The chicken will be done when the internal temperature is at least 165°F.

3 Line a baking sheet with aluminum foil. Place drumsticks on prepared sheet and brush with remaining barbecue sauce. Place in oven and broil 5 minutes to caramelize sauce. Serve warm.

PER SERVING:

CALORIES: 139 | FAT: 6g | SODIUM: 533mg | CARBOHYDRATES: 8g | FIBER: 0g | SUGAR: 6g | PROTEIN: 13g

Spicy Chicken Burgers

Beef isn't the only way to make a perfectly juicy burger. These chicken burgers might be leaner than their red meat counterpart, but they're flavorful, filling, and expertly seasoned. Adobo sauce is a highly seasoned sauce made of chiles and adds a sweet and smoky flavor. It's often found in the international aisle at grocery stores. Most of the time you'll find cans with chipotle peppers in adobo sauce. Simply pour the entire can into the food processor and blend.

Hands-On Time: 10 minutes
Cook Time: 10 minutes

Serves 4

1 pound ground chicken breast
¼ cup chopped pickled jalapeños
¼ cup chopped red onion
½ cup shredded Monterey jack cheese
2 tablespoons adobo sauce
¼ cup panko bread crumbs
1 teaspoon salt
¼ teaspoon ground black pepper
1 cup water
4 burger buns
4 (1-ounce) slices pepper jack cheese

1   In a large bowl, mix chicken, jalapeños, onion, Monterey jack, adobo sauce, bread crumbs, salt, and pepper until well combined. Form mixture into four patties.

2   Pour water into an Instant Pot® and place a steamer basket in the pot, then place patties in basket. Place the lid on the Instant Pot® and click into place to close.

3   Press the Pressure Cook button and adjust the timer to 10 minutes. When the timer beeps, let the pressure release naturally for 5 minutes, then quick-release any remaining pressure until float valve drops. Unlock lid. When done, burgers should have an internal temperature of at least 165°F. Place each burger on a bun and top with pepper jack. Serve warm.

PER SERVING:

CALORIES: 427 | **FAT:** 17g | **SODIUM:** 1,339mg | **CARBOHYDRATES:** 29g | **FIBER:** 2g | **SUGAR:** 4g | **PROTEIN:** 38g

Pesto Chicken

Pesto adds a fresh, tasty flavor to food, and chicken is no exception. Sometimes chicken can feel repetitive and bland, but a simple jar of pesto can really kick things up a notch.

Hands-On Time: 5 minutes
Cook Time: 17 minutes

Serves 4

2 tablespoons olive oil
1 pound boneless, skinless chicken breasts, cut into 1" cubes
1 teaspoon salt
¼ teaspoon ground black pepper
1 cup basil pesto
½ cup chicken broth
½ pint grape tomatoes, halved
½ cup grated Parmesan cheese

SERVING OPTIONS

You can enjoy this dish by itself or over pasta. Penne, bow ties, or linguine are all delicious with this flavorful and easy dish. You can also enjoy it over zucchini noodles or spaghetti squash for a low-carb version.

1 Press the Sauté button on an Instant Pot® and allow to heat until the display reads "Hot." Add olive oil and chicken to the pot. Sprinkle chicken with salt and pepper. Sauté chicken until no pink remains and the internal temperature is at least 165°F, about 7 minutes. Add pesto and broth. Press the Cancel button.

2 Place the lid on the Instant Pot® and click into place to close. Press the Pressure Cook button and adjust the timer to 10 minutes.

3 When the timer beeps, quick-release the pressure until float valve drops. Unlock lid. Stir in tomatoes and sprinkle with Parmesan. Serve warm.

PER SERVING:

CALORIES: 360 | FAT: 33g | SODIUM: 1,483mg | CARBOHYDRATES: 8g | FIBER: 1g | SUGAR: 3g | PROTEIN: 7g

Butter Chicken

This Indian-inspired dish is tender and flavorful and is perfectly complemented by a side of Long-Grain White Rice (see recipe in Chapter 4). If you've never had Butter Chicken, you're in for a treat. The sauce is flavored with garam masala, which is a warm spice blend that has cinnamon, cumin, and peppercorn.

Hands-On Time: 10 minutes
Cook Time: 20 minutes 30 seconds

Serves 6

1 tablespoon olive oil
½ medium yellow onion, peeled and finely chopped
2 cloves garlic, peeled and finely minced
1 tablespoon tomato paste
1½ teaspoons garam masala
1 teaspoon smoked paprika
1 teaspoon salt
½ teaspoon ground cumin
¼ teaspoon ground black pepper
¼ teaspoon ground ginger
⅛ teaspoon ground cinnamon
1 (8-ounce) can tomato sauce
½ cup chicken broth
1½ pounds boneless, skinless chicken breasts
8 tablespoons salted butter
½ cup canned full-fat coconut milk
2 tablespoons cornstarch

1 Press the Sauté button on an Instant Pot® and allow to heat until the display reads "Hot." Add olive oil and onion to the pot and sauté 2 minutes until onion softens. Add garlic and sauté 30 seconds. Stir in tomato paste, garam masala, paprika, salt, cumin, pepper, ginger, and cinnamon until a thick paste forms, about 10 seconds. Press the Cancel button.

2 Pour tomato sauce and broth into the pot. Use a wooden spoon to scrape any browned bit from the bottom of the pot. Place chicken in the pot and push it down to make sure it's fully coated with sauce. Place the lid on the Instant Pot® and click into place to close. Press the Pressure Cook button and adjust the timer to 15 minutes. When the timer beeps, quick-release the pressure until float valve drops. Unlock lid.

3 Press the Cancel button, then the Sauté button. When done, chicken should have an internal temperature of at least 165°F. Place chicken on a cutting board and chop into 1" cubes. Add butter and coconut milk to the pot and stir. Carefully scoop ¼ cup sauce into a small bowl and whisk with cornstarch until smooth. Whisk mixture back into sauce in the pot and add chopped chicken. Stirring frequently, cook an additional 3 minutes until sauce thickens. Serve warm.

PER SERVING:

CALORIES: 364 | FAT: 25g | SODIUM: 887mg | CARBOHYDRATES: 7g | FIBER: 1g | SUGAR: 2g | PROTEIN: 26g

Creamy Mushroom Smothered Chicken

The Instant Pot® is an expert sauce cooker, which makes it the perfect appliance for Creamy Mushroom Smothered Chicken. The savory mushrooms add a delicious earthy flavor to this dish, which goes great next to a bowl of Mashed Potatoes (see recipe in Chapter 6).

Hands-On Time: 5 minutes
Cook Time: 24 minutes

Serves 4

2 tablespoons olive oil
½ medium yellow onion, peeled and sliced
1 cup sliced baby bella mushrooms
4 (6-ounce) boneless, skinless chicken breasts
1 teaspoon salt
½ teaspoon ground black pepper
1 teaspoon Italian seasoning
1 (10.5-ounce) can condensed cream of chicken soup
1 (10.5-ounce) can condensed cream of mushroom soup
1 cup chicken broth
1 (1-ounce) packet brown gravy mix
¼ cup heavy cream
3 tablespoons cornstarch
2 tablespoons salted butter

1 Press the Sauté button on an Instant Pot® and allow to heat until the display reads "Hot." Add olive oil, onion, and mushrooms and sauté 2 minutes until vegetables begin to soften. Sprinkle chicken with salt, pepper, and Italian seasoning. Place chicken in the pot and sear 1 minute on each side until golden brown. Press the Cancel button.

2 Pour chicken soup, mushroom soup, and broth into the pot and stir to combine and coat chicken. Use a wooden spoon to scrape any browned bits from the bottom of the pot. Sprinkle gravy mix over top. Place the lid on the Instant Pot® and click into place to close. Press the Pressure Cook button and adjust the timer to 15 minutes.

3 When the timer beeps, quick-release the pressure until float valve drops. Unlock lid. When done, chicken should have an internal temperature of at least 165°F. Press the Cancel button, then the Sauté button. In a small bowl, whisk together cream and cornstarch until combined, then stir mixture into the pot. Stir in butter. Allow sauce to cook 5 minutes, stirring occasionally, until it thickens. Serve warm with sauce and mushrooms on top of each piece of chicken.

PER SERVING:

CALORIES: 545 | FAT: 32g | SODIUM: 2,367mg | CARBOHYDRATES: 22g | FIBER: 4g | SUGAR: 2g | PROTEIN: 41g

Teriyaki Chicken

This is a crowd favorite so simple that even kids can help put it together. Using chicken thighs ensures maximum flavor, and since they cook directly in the sauce, it captures all the chicken flavor. Pair this recipe with steamed rice for a well-rounded and filling meal.

Hands-On Time: 5 minutes
Cook Time: 20 minutes

Serves 4

1 cup chicken broth
½ cup low-sodium soy sauce
¼ cup light brown sugar, packed
1 tablespoon honey
2 cloves garlic, peeled and finely minced
½ teaspoon ground ginger
4 (4-ounce) boneless, skinless chicken thighs
1 teaspoon salt
¼ teaspoon ground black pepper
2 tablespoons water
2 tablespoons cornstarch
1 scallion, trimmed and sliced
1 tablespoon toasted sesame seeds

1 Place broth, soy sauce, brown sugar, and honey in an Instant Pot® and whisk to combine. Whisk in garlic and ginger. Place chicken thighs in the Instant Pot® and turn them twice to fully coat with sauce. Sprinkle with salt and pepper.

2 Place the lid on the Instant Pot® and click into place to close. Press the Pressure Cook button and adjust the timer to 15 minutes. When the timer beeps, quick-release the pressure until float valve drops. Unlock lid. Press the Cancel button. When done, chicken thighs should have an internal temperature of at least 165°F.

3 Carefully remove chicken thighs from the pot and place on a cutting board. In a small bowl, whisk together water and cornstarch. Press the Sauté button on the Instant Pot® and whisk in cornstarch mixture. Slice chicken and add it back to the pot. Allow sauce to thicken 5 minutes, whisking frequently. The sauce will be done when it's dark brown and coats the chicken in a sticky glaze. Serve warm, topped with scallion and sesame seeds.

PER SERVING:

CALORIES: 276 | **FAT**: 7g | **SODIUM**: 1,719mg | **CARBOHYDRATES**: 27g | **FIBER**: 1g | **SUGAR**: 20g | **PROTEIN**: 24g

Cheesy Chicken and Rice

This creamy, cheesy dish is a bowl of comfort that leaves you feeling warm and satisfied. The ingredients are simple, but they taste great and make the perfect springboard for your own twist. Feel free to add a bag of your favorite frozen vegetables, such as broccoli or Normandy blend.

Hands-On Time: 10 minutes
Cook Time: 9 minutes

Serves 4

2 tablespoons olive oil
1 pound boneless, skinless chicken breasts, cut into ½" cubes
1 teaspoon salt
¼ teaspoon ground black pepper
½ medium white onion, peeled and chopped
2 cups chicken broth
1 cup long-grain white rice, rinsed and drained
½ cup whole milk
1 cup shredded sharp Cheddar cheese

1 Press the Sauté button on an Instant Pot® and allow to heat until the display reads "Hot." Add olive oil and chicken to the pot and sprinkle with salt and pepper. Sauté 5 minutes until chicken is fully cooked and reaches an internal temperature of at least 165°F. Add onion to the pot and sauté 1 minute. Pour in broth and use a wooden spoon to scrape the browned bits from the bottom of the pot.

2 Press the Cancel button and stir in rice. Place the lid on the Instant Pot® and click into place to close. Press the Pressure Cook button and adjust the timer to 3 minutes. When the timer beeps, let the pressure release naturally for 10 minutes, then quick-release any remaining pressure until float valve drops. Unlock lid.

3 Fluff rice with a fork, then stir in milk and Cheddar until creamy. Serve warm.

PER SERVING:

CALORIES: 500 | FAT: 19g | SODIUM: 1,390mg | CARBOHYDRATES: 41g | FIBER: 1g | SUGAR: 3g | PROTEIN: 37g

Avocado Lime Chicken Salad

This twist on chicken salad is big on flavor. If you love avocado, this is a must-try. It's best to use a very ripe, soft avocado so your sauce comes out silky-smooth. The lime enhances all the flavors and makes this dish taste fresh and delicious. Enjoy this salad in a bowl or on top of a tostada for an extra crunch.

Hands-On Time: 10 minutes
Cook Time: 19 minutes

Serves 4

- 3 (6-ounce) boneless, skinless chicken breasts
- 2 teaspoons chili powder
- 1 teaspoon salt
- 1 teaspoon ground cumin
- ½ teaspoon garlic powder
- ¼ teaspoon ground black pepper
- 2 tablespoons olive oil
- ½ cup chicken broth
- ½ cup plus 2 tablespoons lime juice, divided
- ⅔ cup mayonnaise
- 1 large avocado, peeled, pitted, and mashed
- 1 tablespoon grated lime zest
- ¼ cup finely diced red onion
- 1 celery stalk, trimmed and chopped
- ½ medium red bell pepper, seeded and chopped
- ¼ cup chopped fresh cilantro

1 Press the Sauté button on an Instant Pot® and allow to heat until the display reads "Hot." Sprinkle both sides of chicken with chili powder, salt, cumin, garlic powder, and black pepper. Add olive oil and chicken to the pot and sear each side 2 minutes until golden brown.

2 Press the Cancel button. Pour in broth and ½ cup lime juice. Use a wooden spoon to scrape any browned bits from the bottom of the pot. Place the lid on the Instant Pot® and click into place to close. Press the Pressure Cook button and adjust the timer to 15 minutes. When the timer beeps, quick-release the pressure until float valve drops. Unlock lid.

3 When done, chicken should have an internal temperature of at least 165°F. Place chicken on a cutting board and let cool 10 minutes. Cut chicken into ½" cubes. In a large bowl, whisk together mayonnaise and avocado until smooth, then add zest and remaining 2 tablespoons lime juice. Fold in chicken, onion, celery, bell pepper, and cilantro. Chill at least 2 hours before serving.

PER SERVING:

CALORIES: 536 | FAT: 42g | SODIUM: 1,150mg | CARBOHYDRATES: 10g | FIBER: 4g | SUGAR: 2g | PROTEIN: 30g

Hawaiian Chicken

This recipe is perfect for those who enjoy a sweet sauce on their chicken. There's sweetness from the brown sugar and tartness from the orange juice, and the combination makes this recipe loaded with flavor. Hoisin sauce, which can often be found near the soy sauce in the grocery store, adds thickness to the sauce.

Hands-On Time: 5 minutes
Cook Time: 23 minutes

Serves 4

2 tablespoons olive oil
1½ pounds boneless, skinless chicken breasts, cut into ½" cubes
1 medium yellow onion, peeled and diced
2 cloves garlic, peeled and finely minced
1 large red bell pepper, seeded and chopped into ½" pieces
1 large green bell pepper, seeded and chopped into ½" pieces
2 tablespoons brown sugar
¼ cup orange juice
¾ cup chicken broth
1 (20-ounce) can pineapple chunks with juice
2 tablespoons hoisin sauce
¼ cup soy sauce
2 tablespoons water
1 tablespoon cornstarch

1 Press the Sauté button on an Instant Pot® and allow to heat until the display reads "Hot." Add olive oil and chicken to the pot and sauté until no pink remains and chicken reaches an internal temperature of 165°F, about 10 minutes. Add onion and sauté until it begins to soften, about 2 minutes. Add garlic and bell peppers. Sauté 1 minute, then press the Cancel button.

2 Add brown sugar, orange juice, and broth. Use a wooden spoon to stir and remove any browned bits from the bottom of the pot. Stir in pineapple chunks and juice, hoisin sauce, and soy sauce. Place the lid on the Instant Pot® and click into place to close. Press the Pressure Cook button and adjust the timer to 5 minutes. When the timer beeps, quick-release the pressure until float valve drops. Unlock lid.

3 Press the Cancel button, then the Sauté button. In a small bowl, whisk together water and cornstarch, then pour mixture into the Instant Pot® and allow it to thicken, stirring frequently, about 5 minutes. When done, a thick, dark brown sauce will coat chicken. Serve warm.

PER SERVING:

CALORIES: 435 | **FAT:** 12g | **SODIUM:** 1,408mg | **CARBOHYDRATES:** 44g | **FIBER:** 4g | **SUGAR:** 35g | **PROTEIN:** 41g

Italian Chicken Pasta

This creamy dish comes together easily, so it's perfect for weeknight meals. It uses precooked chicken, which is great for leftovers. Each bite is filled with yummy herbs and a delicious creamy sauce.

Hands-On Time: 5 minutes
Cook Time: 5 minutes

Serves 4

2 cups chicken broth

1 (10.5-ounce) can condensed cream of chicken soup

1 (1-ounce) packet dry Italian dressing mix

2 cups shredded cooked chicken breasts

2 cups uncooked bow tie pasta

1 teaspoon Italian seasoning

1 teaspoon salt

4 ounces cream cheese, softened

1 Pour broth into an Instant Pot®, then whisk in soup and Italian dressing mix. Place chicken and pasta in the pot and stir to combine. Sprinkle with Italian seasoning and salt.

2 Place the lid on the Instant Pot® and click into place to close. Press the Pressure Cook button and adjust the timer to 5 minutes. When the timer beeps, quick-release the pressure until float valve drops. Unlock lid.

3 Stir in cream cheese until a smooth sauce forms. Serve warm.

PER SERVING:

CALORIES: 473 | FAT: 17g | SODIUM: 2,573mg | CARBOHYDRATES: 41g | FIBER: 4g | SUGAR: 3g | PROTEIN: 31g

8

Beef and Pork Main Dishes

Like chicken, beef and pork are very common staples that offer variety. They're flavorful, nutritious, and packed with protein. There's no lack of delicious ways that your Instant Pot® can serve up beef and pork, and they're even easier and more enjoyable than ever. With recipes such as Sweet and Spicy Ribs and Philly Cheesesteak Sandwiches, this chapter will help you add filling and mouthwatering meals to your dinner menu.

Easy Cheeseburgers 134

Corned Beef Brisket Sandwiches 135

Sweet and Spicy Ribs 136

Barbecue Short Ribs 137

Cheesy Smoked Sausage and Rice 139

Slow Cooker Beef and Broccoli 140

Hawaiian Pulled Pork Sandwiches 140

Lime Pulled Pork 141

Barbecue Pulled Pork 142

Ginger Orange–Glazed Pork 143

Meatloaf 144

Mississippi Pot Roast 146

Beef Stroganoff 147

Taco-Stuffed Peppers 148

Sloppy Joes 149

Philly Cheesesteak Sandwiches 151

Italian-Style Meatballs in Marinara Sauce 152

Swedish Meatballs 153

Bolognese Sauce 154

Easy Cheeseburgers

Making burgers just got even easier! If you're unsure about using the Instant Pot® for these, you have to try them, because once you bite into the juicy steamed burger, your mind will be forever changed. Besides the fact that they're less messy than cooking on the stovetop, they stay full of moisture and can be stacked for cooking a double batch with ease. Simply double all the ingredients and keep the cook time the same.

Hands-On Time: 10 minutes
Cook Time: 15 minutes

Serves 4

- 1 pound 90/10 ground beef
- 1 teaspoon Worcestershire sauce
- 1 teaspoon salt
- ½ teaspoon ground black pepper
- 1 cup water
- 4 slices American cheese
- 4 hamburger buns

1 Cut four 10½" × 8" aluminum foil pieces. In a large bowl, mix beef and Worcestershire sauce. Form mixture into four patties. Sprinkle both sides of patties with salt and pepper. Wrap each patty individually in foil by placing patty in the center, folding the long edges toward the center, then folding the short edges toward the center to fully enclose the patty.

2 Pour water into an Instant Pot® and place the trivet in the pot, then place burger packets on trivet. Place the lid on the Instant Pot® and click into place to close. Press the Pressure Cook button and adjust the timer to 15 minutes.

3 When the timer beeps, quick-release the pressure until float valve drops. Unlock lid. When done, burgers should have an internal temperature of 160°F for well-done. Carefully transfer each burger to a bun bottom, place 1 cheese slice on each burger, and top with bun tops. Serve warm.

PER SERVING:

CALORIES: 346 | **FAT:** 12g | **SODIUM:** 1,152mg | **CARBOHYDRATES:** 24g | **FIBER:** 1g | **SUGAR:** 4g | **PROTEIN:** 30g

Corned Beef Brisket Sandwiches

These sandwiches are loaded with layers of flavor: juicy beef, melty cheese, spicy dressing, and sauerkraut. This recipe uses pickling spice blend, which you can usually find in the spice aisle at the grocery store. Oftentimes, a packet of spices is included when you buy the brisket, so feel free to use that instead.

Hands-On Time: 10 minutes
Cook Time: 1 hour 18 minutes

Serves 8

- 1½ cups beef broth
- 1 medium yellow onion, peeled and sliced
- 1 (3-pound) flat-cut corned beef brisket
- 2 tablespoons pickling spice blend
- 1 teaspoon salt
- ½ teaspoon ground black pepper
- 16 slices rye bread
- 8 (1-ounce) slices Swiss cheese
- ½ cup sauerkraut
- 1 cup Russian dressing
- 16 dill pickle slices

1 Pour broth into an Instant Pot® and add onion. Place the trivet in the pot, then place brisket on trivet (fat side down). Rub pickling spices into meat, then sprinkle with salt and pepper. Place the lid on the Instant Pot® and click into place to close. Press the Pressure Cook button and adjust the timer to 75 minutes. When the timer beeps, let the pressure release naturally for 15 minutes, then quick-release any remaining pressure until float valve drops. Unlock lid.

2 To assemble sandwiches, transfer brisket to a cutting board and shred with two forks. Place slices of bread on 2 large ungreased baking sheets. Place even amounts of meat on 8 slices of bread, then top meat with 1 slice of cheese, leaving 8 slices of bread plain. Place sheet in oven and broil 3 minutes until cheese is melted and bread is toasted.

3 Remove sheet from oven and top melted cheese with even amounts of sauerkraut and 2 pickle slices per sandwich. Spread 2 tablespoons Russian dressing on each plain slice of bread, then place on bread pieces layered with meat, cheese, sauerkraut, and pickles to top sandwiches. Serve warm.

PER SERVING:

CALORIES: 584 | **FAT:** 29g | **SODIUM:** 2,538mg | **CARBOHYDRATES:** 36g | **FIBER:** 5g | **SUGAR:** 4g | **PROTEIN:** 35g

Sweet and Spicy Ribs

There's nothing quite like tender ribs that easily fall off the bone, and your Instant Pot® gives you all that classic barbecue flavor in a fraction of the time! These ultra-tender ribs are perfect when slathered in your favorite sauce alongside a delicious bowl of creamy potato salad.

Hands-On Time: 10 minutes
Cook Time: 35 minutes

Serves 4

- 1 (2-pound) rack pork back ribs
- 1 teaspoon salt
- ½ teaspoon ground black pepper
- ½ teaspoon garlic powder
- 1 teaspoon ground cayenne pepper
- ½ cup light brown sugar, packed
- ¼ cup apple cider vinegar
- 1 cup water
- 1 cup barbecue sauce

1 Remove the membrane from the underside of ribs. In a medium bowl, mix salt, black pepper, garlic powder, cayenne pepper, and brown sugar. Rub mixture evenly over both sides of ribs.

2 Pour vinegar and water into an Instant Pot® and place the trivet in the pot, then place ribs on trivet, wrapping them in a cylinder shape to make them fit in the pot. Place the lid on the Instant Pot® and click into place to close. Press the Pressure Cook button and adjust the timer to 30 minutes.

3 Line a baking sheet with aluminum foil. When the timer beeps, allow a full natural release of pressure, about 20 minutes, until float valve drops. Unlock lid. When done, ribs should have an internal temperature of at least 145°F. Transfer ribs to prepared sheet. Brush each side with barbecue sauce, then place in oven and broil 5 minutes until sauce has caramelized. Serve warm.

PER SERVING:

CALORIES: 733 | FAT: 36g | SODIUM: 1,485mg | CARBOHYDRATES: 60g | FIBER: 1g | SUGAR: 51g | PROTEIN: 40g

Barbecue Short Ribs

Short ribs come from the chuck area of the cow. They can be tough when cooked too quickly. The trick is to treat them with the care of a cheaper cut of roast and cook slowly. Once you bite into these fall-off-the-bone short ribs, you'll be so glad you took the extra time and patience. The pineapple juice adds acidity and helps the flavors get deep into the meat. If you want to caramelize the sauce, place the ribs on a foil-lined baking sheet and broil in the oven 4 minutes as the last step.

Hands-On Time: 10 minutes
Cook Time: 49 minutes

Serves 4

2 pounds beef short ribs
1 teaspoon salt
½ teaspoon ground black pepper
½ teaspoon garlic powder
¼ teaspoon onion powder
1 cup pineapple juice
1 cup water
1¼ cups barbecue sauce, divided

1 Press the Sauté button on an Instant Pot® and allow to heat until the display reads "Hot." Sprinkle ribs with salt, pepper, garlic powder, and onion powder. Place ribs in the pot and sear 1 minute on each side. Press the Cancel button.

2 Pour pineapple juice into the pot and use a wooden spoon to scrape the browned bits from the bottom. Add water to the pot, then pour 1 cup barbecue sauce over ribs. Place the lid on the Instant Pot® and click into place to close. Press the Pressure Cook button and adjust the timer to 45 minutes.

3 When the timer beeps, let the pressure release naturally for 15 minutes, then quick-release any remaining pressure until float valve drops. Unlock lid. When done, ribs should have an internal temperature of at least 160°F; meat will be very tender, and bones will easily separate from meat. Brush remaining ¼ cup barbecue sauce over ribs. Serve warm.

PER SERVING:

CALORIES: 496 | **FAT:** 24g | **SODIUM:** 961mg | **CARBOHYDRATES:** 13g | **FIBER:** 0g | **SUGAR:** 10g | **PROTEIN:** 46g

Cheesy Smoked Sausage and Rice

If you love a warm bowl of rice and sausage, try this cheesy spin on Cajun rice. It's a complete meal. with vegetables that are super filling, and it comes together in no time. This meal also reheats well in the microwave, which makes it great for meal prep.

Hands-On Time: 10 minutes
Cook Time: 6 minutes

Serves 4

14 ounces smoked sausage, sliced into ¼"-thick slices
½ medium white onion, peeled and chopped
1 medium carrot, peeled and diced
½ cup canned diced tomatoes, drained
1 tablespoon tomato paste
½ teaspoon salt
¼ teaspoon ground black pepper
1 teaspoon chili powder
½ teaspoon ground cumin
½ teaspoon paprika
2 cups chicken broth
1 cup long-grain white rice, rinsed and drained
1 cup shredded sharp Cheddar cheese

1 Press the Sauté button on an Instant Pot® and allow to heat until the display reads "Hot." Add sausage, onion, and carrot. Sauté 3 minutes until vegetables begin to soften and sausage begins to brown.

2 Press the Cancel button and add diced tomatoes, tomato paste, salt, pepper, chili powder, cumin, and paprika. Stir to combine. Pour broth into the pot and use a wooden spoon to scrape any browned bits off the bottom. Stir in rice.

3 Place the lid on the Instant Pot® and click into place to close. Press the Pressure Cook button and adjust the timer to 3 minutes. When the timer beeps, let the pressure release naturally for 10 minutes, then quick-release any remaining pressure until float valve drops. Unlock lid. Stir in Cheddar until well combined. Serve warm.

PER SERVING:

CALORIES: 615 | FAT: 33g | SODIUM: 1,894mg | CARBOHYDRATES: 46g | FIBER: 2g | SUGAR: 3g | PROTEIN: 24g

Slow Cooker Beef and Broccoli

This takeout favorite is easy to make at home. Add a side of rice for a more filling meal.

Hands-On Time: 10 minutes
Cook Time: 4 hours

Serves 6

2 pounds sirloin steak, thinly sliced
½ teaspoon ground black pepper
1¼ cups beef broth, divided
½ cup low-sodium soy sauce
¼ cup light brown sugar, packed
2 cups broccoli florets
2 tablespoons cornstarch

1 Place steak, pepper, 1 cup broth, soy sauce, and brown sugar in an Instant Pot® and stir to combine. Place a glass slow cooker lid on the pot. Press the Slow Cook button and adjust the timer to 3½ hours.

2 When the timer beeps, remove lid, add broccoli to the pot, and stir. In a small bowl, mix remaining ¼ cup broth with cornstarch, then stir mixture into the pot.

3 Place the lid back on the pot and add 30 minutes of slow cook time. When done, beef and broccoli will be tender. Serve warm.

PER SERVING:

CALORIES: 387 | FAT: 16g | SODIUM: 822mg | CARBOHYDRATES: 16g | FIBER: 1g | SUGAR: 11g | PROTEIN: 35g

Hawaiian Pulled Pork Sandwiches

If you're a fan of cabbage, top these sandwiches with a bagged slaw mix for a bit of crunch.

Hands-On Time: 10 minutes
Cook Time: 40 minutes

Serves 6

1 cup pineapple juice
1 cup diced pineapple
½ cup low-sodium soy sauce
½ medium white onion, peeled and chopped
1 teaspoon salt
½ teaspoon ground black pepper
2 cloves garlic, peeled and finely minced
1 (3-pound) pork back roast, cut into 3" cubes
6 Hawaiian burger buns

1 Place all ingredients except buns in an Instant Pot®. Place the lid on the Instant Pot® and click into place to close. Press the Pressure Cook button and adjust the timer to 40 minutes.

2 When the timer beeps, allow a full natural release of pressure until float valve drops. Unlock lid. When done, pork should have an internal temperature of at least 145°F and shred easily.

3 Use two forks to shred pork. Serve warm with sauce on buns.

PER SERVING:

CALORIES: 503 | FAT: 12g | SODIUM: 1,154mg | CARBOHYDRATES: 38g | FIBER: 1g | SUGAR: 18g | PROTEIN: 53g

Lime Pulled Pork

Cooking meat in broth imparts more flavor than cooking it in plain water does, and adding acidity allows the protein fibers to break down, resulting in a more tender and flavorful meat. If you love lime, this recipe is for you. Enjoy this deliciously seasoned dish in a bowl, in a burrito, or on corn tortillas with sliced avocado and cheese.

Hands-On Time: 10 minutes
Cook Time: 40 minutes

Serves 6

1 cup chicken broth
½ cup lime juice
3 pounds boneless pork roast, cut into 3" cubes
1 tablespoon chili powder
1 tablespoon ground cumin
2 teaspoons garlic powder
2 teaspoons salt
½ teaspoon ground black pepper
¼ cup chopped fresh cilantro
1 medium lime, cut into wedges

1 Pour broth and lime juice into an Instant Pot®. Place pork roast in the pot and sprinkle with chili powder, cumin, garlic powder, salt, and pepper. Place the lid on the Instant Pot® and click into place to close.

2 Press the Pressure Cook button and adjust the timer to 40 minutes. When the timer beeps, allow a full natural release of pressure, about 20 minutes, until float valve drops. Unlock lid. When done, pork should have an internal temperature of at least 145°F and shred easily.

3 Shred pork using two forks. Sprinkle cilantro on top of pork. Serve warm with lime wedges.

PER SERVING:

CALORIES: 349 | **FAT:** 13g | **SODIUM:** 1,012mg | **CARBOHYDRATES:** 3g | **FIBER:** 1g | **SUGAR:** 1g | **PROTEIN:** 47g

Barbecue Pulled Pork

This is a classic meal that the whole family can enjoy. The pork comes out tender and coated in savory sauce. Make this dish a part of a picnic plate with potatoes, corn, and macaroni and cheese, or use it to make pulled pork nachos.

Hands-On Time: 10 minutes
Cook Time: 40 minutes

Serves 6

1 medium yellow onion, peeled and cut into quarters
2 cups barbecue sauce
1 tablespoon Worcestershire sauce
½ cup chicken broth
1 (3-pound) pork roast
¼ cup light brown sugar, packed
1 tablespoon chili powder
1 teaspoon garlic powder
1 teaspoon salt
½ teaspoon ground black pepper

MAKE IT SPICY!

If you're a fan of spicy food, add some pickled jalapeños to this dish. You can also use spicy barbecue sauce for an extra burst of heat and flavor.

1 Place onion, barbecue sauce, Worcestershire sauce, and broth in an Instant Pot®. Place roast in the pot and use tongs to coat each side of roast in sauce. Sprinkle brown sugar, chili powder, garlic powder, salt, and pepper over top of roast.

2 Place the lid on the Instant Pot® and click into place to close. Press the Pressure Cook button and adjust the timer to 40 minutes. When the timer beeps, allow a full natural release of pressure, about 20 minutes, until float valve drops. Unlock lid. When done, pork should have an internal temperature of at least 145°F.

3 Use two forks to shred meat, then let sit in warm sauce 10 minutes. Serve warm.

PER SERVING:

CALORIES: 541 | **FAT:** 13g | **SODIUM:** 1,591mg | **CARBOHYDRATES:** 50g | **FIBER:** 1g | **SUGAR:** 41g | **PROTEIN:** 47g

Ginger Orange–Glazed Pork

Pork tenderloin is often underutilized, but it's a lean cut of meat and works great on a budget. This juicy tenderloin cooks quickly in the Instant Pot® and is then glazed in a flavorful sauce. Try this pork sliced on top of steamed rice.

Hands-On Time: 10 minutes
Cook Time: 10 minutes

Serves 6

2 pounds pork tenderloin
½ cup light brown sugar, packed
½ cup orange juice
½ cup low-sodium soy sauce
1 teaspoon ground ginger
½ teaspoon salt
¼ teaspoon ground black pepper
2 tablespoons cornstarch

1 Place pork tenderloin in an Instant Pot® and sprinkle brown sugar over pork. Pour orange juice and soy sauce into the pot. Sprinkle pork with ginger, salt, and pepper. Place the lid on the Instant Pot® and click into place to close.

2 Press the Pressure Cook button and adjust the timer to 5 minutes. When the timer beeps, allow a full natural release of pressure until float valve drops. Unlock lid. When done, pork should have an internal temperature of at least 145°F.

3 Remove pork from the Instant Pot® and set aside on a large plate. Press the Cancel button, then the Sauté button. Whisk cornstarch into liquid that remains in the pot. Stirring frequently, allow sauce to thicken, about 5 minutes. Brush pork with thickened sauce, slice, and serve warm.

PER SERVING:

CALORIES: 263 | **FAT:** 4g | **SODIUM:** 1,053mg | **CARBOHYDRATES:** 26g | **FIBER:** 0g | **SUGAR:** 21g | **PROTEIN:** 29g

Meatloaf

This classic comfort dish steams perfectly in the Instant Pot®. Pair it with steamed vegetables and petite golden potatoes. For your own twist, try swapping ketchup with your favorite barbecue or chili sauce. For a caramelized top, open the aluminum foil packet at the very end and place it on a baking sheet. Broil for 5 minutes until the top begins to caramelize and turn glossy.

Hands-On Time: 10 minutes
Cook Time: 25 minutes

Serves 6

2 pounds 80/20 ground beef
½ medium yellow onion, peeled and finely chopped
1 large egg
¾ cup Italian-style bread crumbs
2 teaspoons Italian seasoning
½ teaspoon garlic powder
1 teaspoon salt
½ teaspoon ground black pepper
2 tablespoons light brown sugar, packed
½ cup ketchup
1 teaspoon apple cider vinegar
1 cup water

1   In a large bowl, mix beef, onion, egg, and bread crumbs. Add Italian seasoning, garlic powder, salt, and pepper and mix until well combined. Form mixture into a 6" × 4" loaf shape, about 1" tall. In a small bowl, whisk together brown sugar, ketchup, and vinegar, then brush mixture over loaf.

2   Wrap loaf tightly in aluminum foil. Pour water into an Instant Pot® and place the trivet in the pot, then place wrapped loaf on trivet. Place the lid on the Instant Pot® and click into place to close. Press the Pressure Cook button and adjust the timer to 25 minutes.

3   When the timer beeps, let the pressure release naturally for 10 minutes, then quick-release any remaining pressure until float valve drops. Unlock lid. When done, meatloaf will have an internal temperature of at least 160°F. Remove from pot and allow to rest 10 minutes before slicing. Serve warm.

PER SERVING:

CALORIES: 380 | FAT: 16g | SODIUM: 853mg | CARBOHYDRATES: 22g | FIBER: 1g | SUGAR: 10g | PROTEIN: 30g

Mississippi Pot Roast

Nothing says comfort food quite like pot roast. If you've never made one, this recipe is an excellent place to start. Underseasoning and overcooking can be the most frustrating part of cooking a roast, but this recipe takes out the guesswork by using just two packets of seasoning mixes.

Hands-On Time: 5 minutes
Cook Time: 1 hour

Serves 8

2 cups beef broth
1 (3-pound) chuck roast, fat trimmed
1 (1-ounce) packet dry au jus seasoning
1 (1-ounce) packet dry ranch seasoning
4 tablespoons salted butter, sliced
½ cup sliced pepperoncini peppers

GRAVY

The leftover juice in the Instant Pot® is perfect for pouring over the roast to serve. You can leave it as is, or strain it and then return it to the Instant Pot®. Press the Sauté button, then whisk in a slurry of ¼ cup milk and 1 tablespoon all-purpose flour. Continue whisking until mixture thickens, about 2 minutes. Pour into a gravy boat to serve.

1 Pour broth into an Instant Pot®, then place roast in the pot. Sprinkle au jus and ranch seasoning packets over roast. Place sliced butter on top of roast and scatter peppers around the pot.

2 Place the lid on the Instant Pot® and click into place to close. Press the Pressure Cook button and adjust the timer to 1 hour. When the timer beeps, allow a full natural release of pressure, about 20 minutes, until float valve drops. Unlock lid.

3 When done, roast should have an internal temperature of at least 160°F and meat will easily pull apart. Slice or shred to serve.

PER SERVING:

CALORIES: 250 | **FAT:** 7g | **SODIUM:** 786mg | **CARBOHYDRATES:** 3g | **FIBER:** 0g | **SUGAR:** 0g | **PROTEIN:** 38g

Beef Stroganoff

Stew meat is the most tender when it's cooked for a long time. The Instant Pot® gives you all the tenderness of low and slow cooking in less than 30 minutes. The stew meat becomes tender and covered in a delicious creamy sauce. If you can't find stew meat, you can swap it for an equal amount of ground beef or sliced sirloin.

Hands-On Time: 5 minutes
Cook Time: 14 minutes

Serves 4

2 tablespoons salted butter
1 tablespoon olive oil
1 teaspoon salt
½ teaspoon ground black pepper
1 teaspoon Italian seasoning
1 pound beef stew meat, cut into ½" pieces
1 medium onion, peeled and chopped
8 ounces cremini mushrooms, sliced
2 tablespoons all-purpose flour
2 cloves garlic, peeled and finely minced
1½ cups beef broth
½ cup sour cream

1 Press the Sauté button on an Instant Pot® and allow to heat until the display reads "Hot." Add butter and olive oil to the pot. Sprinkle salt, pepper, and Italian seasoning on meat and place in the pot. Sear meat, turning every 45 seconds, until browned. Add onion and mushrooms to the pot. Sauté 2 minutes until vegetables begin to soften.

2 Sprinkle flour and garlic into the pot, sauté 30 seconds, then pour in broth. Use a wooden spoon to scrape the browned bits from the bottom of the pot.

3 Press the Cancel button. Place the lid on the Instant Pot® and click into place to close. Press the Pressure Cook button and adjust the timer to 10 minutes. When the timer beeps, let the pressure release naturally for 10 minutes, then quick-release any remaining pressure until float valve drops. Unlock lid. Stir in sour cream until a thick sauce forms. Serve warm.

PER SERVING:

CALORIES: 326 | FAT: 19g | SODIUM: 1,070mg | CARBOHYDRATES: 10g | FIBER: 1g | SUGAR: 3g | PROTEIN: 29g

Taco-Stuffed Peppers

Taco flavors and bell peppers are a great match, and this recipe brings them together in a yummy dish. With only six ingredients, this easy-to-make meal will leave you feeling satisfied. Try these stuffed peppers with sour cream, guacamole, or sliced scallions.

Hands-On Time: 10 minutes
Cook Time: 14 minutes

Serves 6

1 pound 70/30 ground beef
1 (10-ounce) can diced tomatoes and green chiles
½ medium white onion, peeled and diced
1 (1-ounce) packet taco seasoning
6 large green bell peppers, tops removed and seeded
¾ cup shredded Mexican cheese blend
1 cup water

1 Press the Sauté button on an Instant Pot® and allow to heat until the display reads "Hot." Break beef into small pieces and add to the pot. Crumble and sauté 7 minutes until no pink remains. Drain grease. Press the Cancel button.

2 Add diced tomatoes and chiles, onion, and taco seasoning. Stir to combine and let cook 3 minutes. Scoop ½ cup mixture into each bell pepper. Sprinkle 2 tablespoons cheese on top of each pepper.

3 Cut six 7" × 7" pieces of aluminum foil. Wrap each pepper tightly in foil. Pour water into the Instant Pot® and place the trivet in the pot, then place wrapped peppers on trivet. Place the lid on the Instant Pot® and click into place to close. Press the Pressure Cook button and adjust the timer to 4 minutes. When the timer beeps, quick-release the pressure until float valve drops. Unlock lid. Serve warm.

PER SERVING:

CALORIES: 234 | FAT: 11g | SODIUM: 580mg | CARBOHYDRATES: 13g | FIBER: 4g | SUGAR: 6g | PROTEIN: 17g

Sloppy Joes

No need to use premade sloppy joe sauce; you can easily make it from scratch! Each sandwich is filled with chunks of meat and vegetables and a yummy, sweet tomato sauce. You'll be so amazed how fresh this meal tastes that you might never go back to the canned sauce again.

Hands-On Time: 10 minutes
Cook Time: 17 minutes

Serves 6

- 1 pound 70/30 ground beef
- ½ medium yellow onion, peeled and diced
- ½ medium green bell pepper, seeded and chopped
- 1 tablespoon tomato paste
- 1 tablespoon light brown sugar, packed
- ½ teaspoon Worcestershire sauce
- ½ teaspoon salt
- ¼ teaspoon ground black pepper
- 1 cup beef broth
- 1 (8-ounce) can tomato sauce
- 1 tablespoon cornstarch
- 6 hamburger buns

1 Press the Sauté button on an Instant Pot® and allow to heat until the display reads "Hot." Add beef and sauté until no pink remains, about 7 minutes. Add onion, bell pepper, tomato paste, brown sugar, and Worcestershire sauce to the pot. Stir and sauté 2 minutes until vegetables begin to soften.

2 Sprinkle salt and black pepper into the pot, then pour in broth and tomato sauce. Press the Cancel button. Place the lid on the Instant Pot® and click into place to close. Press the Pressure Cook button and adjust the timer to 5 minutes. When the timer beeps, quick-release the pressure until float valve drops. Unlock lid.

3 Press the Cancel button, then the Sauté button. Whisk in cornstarch and allow mixture to thicken 3 minutes, stirring occasionally. Place ½ cup mixture on each bun. Serve warm.

PER SERVING:

CALORIES: 416 | FAT: 23g | SODIUM: 755mg | CARBOHYDRATES: 28g | FIBER: 2g | SUGAR: 7g | PROTEIN: 16g

Philly Cheesesteak Sandwiches

A great way to stretch the value of steak is to make it into sandwiches. The jalapeño juice adds a ton of flavor to the meat without any of the heat. If you want to melt the provolone cheese at the end, place sandwiches on a foil-lined baking sheet and broil in oven 2 minutes.

Hands-On Time: 10 minutes
Cook Time: 11 minutes

Serves 4

2 tablespoons olive oil
1 pound thinly sliced sirloin steak
1 medium green bell pepper, seeded and sliced into ¼"-thick slices
1 medium red bell pepper, seeded and sliced into ¼"-thick slices
½ medium white onion, peeled and sliced into ½"-thick slices
½ teaspoon seasoned salt
¼ teaspoon salt
¼ teaspoon ground black pepper
¼ cup jalapeño juice from a jar of pickled jalapeños
¾ cup beef broth
4 hoagie rolls, toasted
⅓ cup sliced banana peppers
4 (1-ounce) slices provolone cheese

1 Press the Sauté button on an Instant Pot® and allow to heat until the display reads "Hot." Add olive oil and steak to the pot. Sauté 5 minutes until meat is no longer pink. Add bell peppers and onion and continue sautéing until vegetables begin to soften, about 1 minute.

2 Sprinkle seasoned salt, salt, and black pepper into the pot. Pour in jalapeño juice and broth, then press the Cancel button. Place the lid on the Instant Pot® and click into place to close. Press the Pressure Cook button and adjust the timer to 5 minutes. When the timer beeps, let the pressure release naturally for 4 minutes, then quick-release any remaining pressure until float valve drops. Unlock lid.

3 Use a slotted spoon or tongs to pick up meat and vegetables and place even amounts on each roll. Top with banana peppers, then provolone. Serve warm.

PER SERVING:

CALORIES: 625 | FAT: 32g | SODIUM: 689mg | CARBOHYDRATES: 41g | FIBER: 4g | SUGAR: 6g | PROTEIN: 41g

CHEESE

This recipe uses provolone, which is mild and great for melting. Feel free to use any cheese of your choice. You may also omit the sliced cheese and use processed Cheddar cheese such as Cheez Whiz Cheese Sauce.

Italian-Style Meatballs in Marinara Sauce

This classic dish never disappoints. It's perfect for weeknights, either on its own or with a side of pasta. By cooking the meatballs directly in the sauce, the flavors marry and create an herb-filled meal. For even more freshness, add sliced basil on top.

Hands-On Time: 10 minutes
Cook Time: 11 minutes

Serves 5

1 pound 80/20 ground beef
1 large egg
½ cup Italian-style bread crumbs
2 teaspoons Italian seasoning
½ teaspoon garlic powder
½ teaspoon salt
¼ teaspoon ground black pepper
2 tablespoons olive oil
2 cups marinara sauce
¼ cup grated Parmesan cheese

1 In a large bowl, mix beef, egg, bread crumbs, Italian seasoning, garlic powder, salt, and pepper until well combined. Using 1 table-spoon mixture per meatball, roll into twenty meatballs and set on a plate.

2 Press the Sauté button on an Instant Pot® and allow to heat until the display reads "Hot." Add olive oil to the pot, then place meatballs in the pot and brown, about 20 seconds per side. Press the Cancel button. Pour marinara sauce into the pot and use a wooden spoon to gently scrape the bottom and loosen any browned bits. Place the lid on the Instant Pot® and click into place to close.

3 Press the Pressure Cook button and adjust the timer to 9 minutes. When the timer beeps, let the pressure release naturally for 5 minutes, then quick-release any remaining pressure until float valve drops. Unlock lid. When done, meatballs will have an internal temperature of at least 160°F. Sprinkle with Parmesan. Serve warm.

PER SERVING:

CALORIES: 411 | FAT: 24g | SODIUM: 999mg | CARBOHYDRATES: 17g | FIBER: 3g | SUGAR: 7g | PROTEIN: 22g

Swedish Meatballs

These creamy meatballs are perfect for dinner and can even be used as appetizers. They're a great alternative to tomato-based sauces with meatballs. If you enjoy beef Stroganoff, you might enjoy these flavorful meatballs with a similar flavor profile.

Hands-On Time: 10 minutes
Cook Time: 11 minutes

Serves 4

1 pound 70/30 ground beef
1 teaspoon salt
¼ cup Italian-style bread crumbs
¼ teaspoon ground allspice
¼ teaspoon ground nutmeg
¼ teaspoon ground black pepper
1 large egg yolk
¼ medium yellow onion, peeled and finely chopped
2 cups beef broth
2 tablespoons all-purpose flour
1 cup half-and-half
½ tablespoon Worcestershire sauce
1 teaspoon Dijon mustard
2 tablespoons cornstarch

1   In a large bowl, mix beef, salt, bread crumbs, allspice, nutmeg, pepper, egg yolk, and onion until well combined. Roll mixture into sixteen meatballs, about 1½" in diameter, and set on a large plate.

2   Pour broth into an Instant Pot® and whisk in flour, then add meatballs. Place the lid on the Instant Pot® and click into place to close. Press the Pressure Cook button and adjust the timer to 8 minutes. When the timer beeps, quick-release the pressure until float valve drops. Unlock lid.

3   Press the Cancel button, then the Sauté button. Carefully remove meatballs from the pot and set aside in a bowl briefly. When done, meatballs should have an internal temperature of at least 160°F. Whisk half-and-half, Worcestershire sauce, mustard, and cornstarch together in the pot until smooth. Continue whisking 3 minutes until sauce thickens. Return meatballs to sauce and gently toss to coat. Serve warm.

PER SERVING:

CALORIES: 541 | FAT: 39g | SODIUM: 1,281mg | CARBOHYDRATES: 16g | FIBER: 1g | SUGAR: 4g | PROTEIN: 22g

Bolognese Sauce

Meat sauce is great to have on hand for quick meals. You can enjoy it with any pasta, or even spaghetti squash. It's easy to make and has a ton of flavor. This delicious tomato-based sauce is finished with a touch of cream that reduces the acidity and pulls all the sauce flavors together.

Hands-On Time: 10 minutes
Cook Time: 23 minutes

Serves 6

- 1 pound 70/30 ground beef
- ¼ pound ground Italian sausage
- 1 medium yellow onion, peeled and chopped
- 1 medium carrot, peeled and grated
- ½ teaspoon salt
- ¼ teaspoon ground black pepper
- 2 tablespoons tomato paste
- 2 cloves garlic, peeled and finely minced
- ½ teaspoon oregano
- 1 (28-ounce) can crushed tomatoes
- ½ cup beef broth
- ¼ cup heavy cream
- ¼ cup chopped fresh parsley

1 Press the Sauté button on an Instant Pot® and allow to heat until the display reads "Hot." Crumble beef and sausage and place in the pot. Sear until no pink remains, about 9 minutes. Add onion, carrot, salt, pepper, and tomato paste and sauté until vegetables begin to soften, about 3 minutes.

2 Add garlic and oregano, then pour in crushed tomatoes and broth. Use a wooden spoon to scrape any browned bits off the bottom of the pot. Press the Cancel button. Place the lid on the Instant Pot® and click into place to close. Press the Pressure Cook button and adjust the timer to 10 minutes.

3 When the timer beeps, quick-release the pressure until float valve drops. Unlock lid. Press the Cancel button, then the Sauté button. Stir in cream and parsley and cook for 1 additional minute. Serve warm.

PER SERVING:

CALORIES: 374 | FAT: 25g | SODIUM: 432mg | CARBOHYDRATES: 14g | FIBER: 4g | SUGAR: 7g | PROTEIN: 15g

Fish and Seafood Main Dishes

Cooking fish and seafood doesn't have to be intimidating. Most home cooks are wary of trying new seafood dishes because of the preciseness, attention, and experience needed to prepare them properly. This chapter is here to flip that notion on its head.

Even if you've never picked up raw salmon in your life, your Instant Pot® will help take care of the guesswork and bring you the delicate, flavorful, and nutritious meals you and your family won't be able to get enough of. From Honey Garlic–Glazed Salmon to restaurant-quality Lobster Tails, this chapter's recipes will help you explore new flavors and add some variety to your weekly meals.

Lobster Tails 156

Classic Shrimp 157

Snow Crab Legs 157

Cajun Shrimp and Sausage Boil 158

Lemon Dill Salmon 160

Spicy Chili Lime Salmon 161

Honey Garlic–Glazed Salmon 162

Chipotle Lime Shrimp 163

Fish Tacos 165

Mussels 166

Cajun Garlic Butter Cod 167

Creamy Tuscan Salmon 168

Seafood Stock 169

Crab-Stuffed Peppers 170

Tomato Steamed Halibut 172

Lobster Tails

Cooking lobster tails at home might feel a bit intimidating, but they're simpler than you might realize. They cook quickly like other seafood, and they really shine with minimal seasoning. You'll be ready to impress with these fresh, juicy Lobster Tails!

Hands-On Time: 5 minutes
Cook Time: 2 minutes

Serves 4

4 (6-ounce) lobster tails
4 tablespoons salted butter, melted, divided
1 teaspoon Old Bay Seasoning
¼ cup lemon juice, divided
1 cup water
1 teaspoon chopped fresh parsley

1 Prepare lobster tails by carefully cutting down the center of the shells. Open the shells in a butterflied position and gently pull the lobster meat up so it's detached but still sitting inside the shells.

2 Brush each lobster tail with ½ tablespoon butter, then sprinkle each with ¼ teaspoon Old Bay Seasoning. Pour ¼ teaspoon lemon juice over each lobster tail.

3 Pour water into an Instant Pot® and place a steamer basket in the pot, then place lobster tails in basket. Place the lid on the Instant Pot® and click into place to close. Press the Pressure Cook button and adjust the timer to 2 minutes. When the timer beeps, quick-release the pressure until float valve drops. Unlock lid. When done, lobster tails should have an internal temperature of at least 145°F and meat will be opaque white. Sprinkle with parsley, remaining butter, and remaining lemon juice to serve.

PER SERVING:

CALORIES: 180 | **FAT:** 11g | **SODIUM:** 644mg | **CARBOHYDRATES:** 1g | **FIBER:** 0g | **SUGAR:** 0g | **PROTEIN:** 16g

Classic Shrimp

Whether you're dipping Classic Shrimp in cocktail sauce or adding it to your favorite seafood pasta, this go-to recipe is both easy and quick.

Hands-On Time: 5 minutes
Cook Time: 1 minute

Serves 4

1 pound medium shrimp, peeled and deveined
1 cup seafood stock
1 tablespoon Old Bay Seasoning

1 Place all ingredients in an Instant Pot® and stir. Place the lid on the Instant Pot® and click into place to close. Press the Pressure Cook button and adjust the timer to 1 minute.

2 When the timer beeps, quick-release the pressure until float valve drops. Unlock lid.

3 When done, shrimp should be C-shaped and an opaque pink color. Serve immediately.

PER SERVING:

CALORIES: 81 | FAT: 1g | SODIUM: 692mg | CARBOHYDRATES: 1g | FIBER: 0g | SUGAR: 0g | PROTEIN: 16g

Snow Crab Legs

Just sprinkle these crab legs with seasoning and let the Instant Pot® do all the hard work.

Hands-On Time: 5 minutes
Cook Time: 3 minutes

Serves 4

2 cups seafood stock
2 pounds snow crab legs
1 tablespoon Old Bay Seasoning
2 tablespoons salted butter, melted
1 medium lemon, cut into wedges

1 Pour stock into an Instant Pot®, then place crab legs in the pot and sprinkle Old Bay Seasoning over crab legs.

2 Place the lid on the Instant Pot® and click into place to close. Press the Pressure Cook button and adjust the timer to 3 minutes. When the timer beeps, quick-release the pressure until float valve drops. Unlock lid. When done, crab legs should be a bright orange or reddish color.

3 Serve immediately with butter for dipping and lemon wedges to squeeze over leg meat.

PER SERVING:

CALORIES: 142 | FAT: 7g | SODIUM: 635mg | CARBOHYDRATES: 0g | FIBER: 0g | SUGAR: 0g | PROTEIN: 19g

Cajun Shrimp and Sausage Boil

This recipe is great on those days when you need to place everything in the pot and move on to the next task. The key to a good boil is making sure you add enough seasoning to flavor all the different ingredients sufficiently, but don't worry: This recipe has you covered with a spicy Cajun seasoning and the classic Old Bay Seasoning. If you don't have a go-to Cajun seasoning, try Slap Ya Mama seasoning, which is found in most grocery stores in the spice aisle.

Hands-On Time: 10 minutes
Cook Time: 11 minutes 30 seconds

Serves 6

2 tablespoons salted butter

1 medium yellow onion, peeled and chopped

½ pound andouille sausage, sliced into ½"-thick pieces

2 cloves garlic, peeled and finely minced

½ pound baby red potatoes, quartered

2 ears corn, husks and silk removed, each cut into 3 pieces

1 cup seafood stock

2 tablespoons Cajun seasoning blend

½ teaspoon salt

1 teaspoon Old Bay Seasoning

1 pound jumbo shrimp, peeled and deveined

1 Press the Sauté button on an Instant Pot® and allow to heat until the display reads "Hot." Add butter, onion, and sausage. Sauté 3 minutes until onion is softened and sausage begins to brown. Add garlic and sauté 30 seconds, then press the Cancel button.

2 Add potatoes, corn, stock, and Cajun seasoning. Place the lid on the Instant Pot® and click into place to close. Press the Pressure Cook button and adjust the timer to 6 minutes. When the timer beeps, quick-release the pressure until float valve drops. Unlock lid. Press the Cancel button.

3 Sprinkle salt and Old Bay Seasoning on top of shrimp, then place shrimp on top of potatoes and corn. Place the lid back on the pot and click into place to close. Press the Pressure Cook button and adjust the timer to 2 minutes. When the timer beeps, quick-release the pressure until float valve drops. Unlock lid. When done, shrimp will be C-shaped and an opaque pink color. Serve warm.

PER SERVING:

CALORIES: 233 | FAT: 11g | SODIUM: 1,434mg | CARBOHYDRATES: 16g | FIBER: 3g | SUGAR: 3g | PROTEIN: 19g

Lemon Dill Salmon

This simple recipe is a classic for good reason. Lemon and dill always go perfectly with salmon, and these simple flavors are all you need to make this delicious meal. Pair this with a side of steamed rice and green beans.

Hands-On Time: 5 minutes
Cook Time: 3 minutes

Serves 4

1 cup water
4 (5-ounce) salmon fillets
2 tablespoons salted butter, melted
4 teaspoons dried dill
½ teaspoon salt
¼ teaspoon ground black pepper
1 large lemon, sliced

1 Pour water into an Instant Pot® and place a steamer basket in the pot, then place salmon in basket. Brush each fillet with butter.

2 Sprinkle each fillet with dill, salt, and pepper. Place 2 lemon slices on each fillet. Place the lid on the Instant Pot® and click into place to close. Press the Pressure Cook button and adjust the timer to 3 minutes.

3 When the timer beeps, quick-release the pressure until float valve drops. Unlock lid. When done, salmon will flake easily and have an internal temperature of at least 145°F. Serve immediately.

PER SERVING:

CALORIES: 301 | FAT: 19g | SODIUM: 411mg | CARBOHYDRATES: 1g | FIBER: 0g | SUGAR: 0g | PROTEIN: 27g

Spicy Chili Lime Salmon

This flavor-packed recipe is perfect if you're looking for something easy but exciting. This meal is quick enough to make on busy weeknights. The chili garlic sauce gives it lots of spice, and the lime adds a fresh element that brings all the flavors together.

Hands-On Time: 5 minutes
Cook Time: 3 minutes

Serves 4

4 (4-ounce) salmon fillets
1 tablespoon olive oil
1 clove garlic, peeled and minced
2 tablespoons low-sodium soy sauce
1 tablespoon chili garlic sauce
2 teaspoons light brown sugar, packed
½ teaspoon salt
¼ teaspoon ground black pepper
1 teaspoon crushed red pepper
1 medium lime, cut into 8 slices
1 cup water

CHILI GARLIC SAUCE
Huy Fong Chili Garlic Sauce is a great brand to use for this recipe. It's made with simple ingredients and is easily found at most grocery stores in the international food section. Sriracha can be used in its place if you need a substitute. It's thicker than chili garlic sauce but will still add some heat to your dish.

1 Place salmon in a steamer basket. In a small bowl, whisk together olive oil, garlic, soy sauce, chili garlic sauce, and brown sugar.

2 Sprinkle salmon with salt, black pepper, and crushed red pepper, then brush spice mixture generously over each fillet, including the sides. Place 2 lime slices on top of each fillet. Pour water into an Instant Pot® and place basket in pot.

3 Place the lid on the Instant Pot® and click into place to close. Press the Pressure Cook button and adjust the timer to 3 minutes. When the timer beeps, quick-release the pressure until float valve drops. Unlock lid. When done, salmon should be opaque, flake easily, and have an internal temperature of at least 145°F. Serve immediately.

PER SERVING:

CALORIES: 244 | FAT: 14g | SODIUM: 652mg | CARBOHYDRATES: 4g | FIBER: 0g | SUGAR: 3g | PROTEIN: 22g

Honey Garlic–Glazed Salmon

Salmon always tastes delicious when covered in a spicy and sticky sauce. This recipe gives you just that with a spicy honey glaze that goes perfectly with rice or steamed Brussels sprouts.

Hands-On Time: 5 minutes
Cook Time: 3 minutes

Serves 4

4 (5-ounce) salmon fillets
1 tablespoon olive oil
2 cloves garlic, peeled and finely minced
½ teaspoon salt
¼ teaspoon ground black pepper
2 tablespoons lemon juice
¼ cup honey
½ tablespoon sriracha
1 cup water

ADDITIONAL GARNISH

For a fresh element, add sliced scallions before serving. Toasted sesame seeds will also add a bit of crunch to this meal. To make these, simply heat a dry skillet over medium heat. Toast the seeds 3 minutes, stirring constantly, until they turn golden and have a nutty aroma. The seeds can burn easily, so keep a close watch on them.

1 Cut four 8" × 8" pieces of aluminum foil to make foil packets. Place 1 fillet on each piece of foil. Drizzle olive oil over each fillet and sprinkle with garlic, salt, and pepper.

2 In a small bowl, mix lemon juice, honey, and sriracha. Generously brush mixture over each fillet. Fold foil over the fillets toward the center, then fold the ends to completely close packets.

3 Pour water into an Instant Pot® and place the trivet in the pot, then place foil packets on trivet, overlapping as needed. Place the lid on the Instant Pot® and click into place to close. Press the Pressure Cook button and adjust the timer to 3 minutes. When the timer beeps, quick-release the pressure until float valve drops. Unlock lid. When done, salmon should flake easily and have an internal temperature of at least 145°F. Serve immediately, with foil packet sauce poured over each fillet.

PER SERVING:

CALORIES: 283 | **FAT:** 17g | **SODIUM:** 376mg | **CARBOHYDRATES:** 2g | **FIBER:** 0g | **SUGAR:** 1g | **PROTEIN:** 27g

Chipotle Lime Shrimp

If you're a fan of juicy shrimp with tons of flavor, this recipe is for you! These perfectly steamed shrimp make a great meal or poppable appetizer. The smoky chipotle flavor really takes this meal to the next level without much additional preparation, and the adobo sauce and tangy lime juice pair nicely.

Hands-On Time: 5 minutes
Cook Time: 1 minute

Serves 4

1 pound medium shrimp,
    peeled and deveined
2 tablespoons adobo sauce
1 medium lime, juiced
½ teaspoon salt
¼ teaspoon ground black
    pepper
1 clove garlic, peeled and
    finely minced
¼ teaspoon chipotle powder
1 cup water

DEVEINED SHRIMP

Always be sure to either buy deveined shrimp or remove the vein before cooking. The vein, the blueish line running through the shrimp, is the digestive tract. You can easily run a sharp knife on each side and then on the underside to remove. Always be sure to rinse shrimp well afterward.

1 Place shrimp, adobo sauce, lime juice, salt, pepper, garlic, and chipotle powder in a large bowl and toss until shrimp are thoroughly coated.

2 Place shrimp in a 6" round baking pan and cover tightly with aluminum foil. Pour water into an Instant Pot® and place the trivet in the pot, then place pan on trivet. Place the lid on the Instant Pot® and click into place to close. Press the Pressure Cook button and adjust the timer to 1 minute.

3 When the timer beeps, quick-release the pressure until float valve drops. Unlock lid. When done, shrimp should be C-shaped and an opaque pink color. Stir shrimp in sauce and serve immediately.

PER SERVING:

CALORIES: 91 | **FAT:** 1g | **SODIUM:** 978mg | **CARBOHYDRATES:** 3g | **FIBER:** 0g | **SUGAR:** 0g | **PROTEIN:** 16g

Fish Tacos

Making Fish Tacos in the Instant Pot® is super easy and quick. If you have time to make the slaw beforehand, letting it marinate for an hour helps soften the cabbage and marry the flavors, but if you're short on time, don't worry; it's delicious either way.

Hands-On Time: 10 minutes
Cook Time: 5 minutes

Serves 4

1 cup water
16 ounces frozen cod fillets, thawed
1 tablespoon olive oil
1 teaspoon chili powder
½ teaspoon salt
½ teaspoon ground cumin
¼ teaspoon garlic powder
¼ teaspoon ground black pepper
1½ tablespoons grated lime zest
1 tablespoon lime juice
¼ cup mayonnaise
¼ cup sour cream
2 cups shredded green and red cabbage blend
8 (4") white corn tortillas, warmed
2 tablespoons chopped fresh cilantro

1 Pour water into an Instant Pot® and place a steamer basket in the pot. Drizzle cod with olive oil and sprinkle with chili powder, salt, cumin, garlic powder, pepper, and lime zest. Place fillets in basket. Place the lid on the Instant Pot® and click into place to close. Press the Pressure Cook button and adjust the timer to 5 minutes. When the timer beeps, quick-release the pressure until float valve drops. Unlock lid.

2 In a medium bowl, whisk together lime juice, mayonnaise, and sour cream. Fold in cabbage.

3 To assemble tacos, place even amounts of cod on each tortilla, then top with cabbage slaw. Garnish with cilantro. Serve warm.

PER SERVING:

CALORIES: 321 | FAT: 17g | SODIUM: 485mg | CARBOHYDRATES: 17g | FIBER: 3g | SUGAR: 2g | PROTEIN: 23g

CHIPOTLE SAUCE

Chipotle sauce is a flavorful mayonnaise-based sauce that goes well with fish. Make your own by whisking ½ cup mayonnaise with 2 tablespoons adobo sauce and a squeeze of lime juice. Then simply drizzle over tacos.

Mussels

Mussels can be intimidating because they are very delicate and overcook quickly. The good news is, preparing this elegant seafood has never been easier. Steaming them in your Instant Pot® for just a few minutes gives you perfect results every time.

Hands-On Time: 5 minutes
Cook Time: 3 minutes

Serves 4

1 cup seafood stock
4 pounds mussels
1 tablespoon grated lemon zest
1 teaspoon salt
¼ teaspoon ground black pepper
1 (14.5-ounce) can stewed tomatoes

1 Pour stock into an Instant Pot® and place a steamer basket in the pot, then place mussels in basket.

2 Sprinkle mussels with lemon zest, salt, and pepper. Pour tomatoes on top. Place the lid on the Instant Pot® and click into place to close. Press the Pressure Cook button and adjust the timer to 3 minutes.

3 When the timer beeps, let the pressure release naturally for 5 minutes, then quick-release any remaining pressure until float valve drops. Unlock lid. When done, mussels will be open and meat will be firm. Serve warm in a bowl with broth from the pot.

PER SERVING:

CALORIES: 294 | FAT: 5g | SODIUM: 1,437mg | CARBOHYDRATES: 17g | FIBER: 2g | SUGAR: 4g | PROTEIN: 38g

Cajun Garlic Butter Cod

White fish like cod is great to work with because it's so versatile. It can be creamy, classic, or spicy. This recipe mixes a little bit of everything and adds a Cajun kick. This recipe calls for seafood stock to give it more flavor, but if you can't find it, feel free to substitute water, or make the Seafood Stock recipe in this chapter.

Hands-On Time: 5 minutes
Cook Time: 8 minutes 30 seconds

Serves 4

2 tablespoons olive oil
3 cloves garlic, peeled and minced
1 tablespoon Cajun seasoning, divided
1 cup seafood stock
4 (4-ounce) cod fillets
½ teaspoon salt
¼ teaspoon ground black pepper
1 medium lemon, cut into 8 slices
2 tablespoons salted butter
¼ cup heavy whipping cream
1 tablespoon cornstarch

WHITE FISH

White fish varieties like cod, haddock, and tilapia are easily interchangeable in this recipe. They have the same cook time and are all mild-tasting fish. Feel free to switch them out and shop the sales without compromising flavor.

1 Press the Sauté button on an Instant Pot® and allow to heat until the display reads "Hot." Add olive oil, garlic, and 1 teaspoon Cajun seasoning. Sauté 30 seconds, then press the Cancel button.

2 Pour stock into the pot and use a wooden spoon to scrape any browned bits from the bottom. Place a steamer basket in the pot, then place fillets in basket. Sprinkle with salt, pepper, and 1 teaspoon Cajun seasoning. Place 2 lemon slices on each fillet. Place the lid on the Instant Pot® and click into place to close. Press the Pressure Cook button and adjust the timer to 3 minutes. When the timer beeps, quick-release the pressure until float valve drops. Unlock lid. When done, cod should flake easily and have an internal temperature of at least 145°F.

3 Remove basket and set aside. Press the Cancel button, then the Sauté button. Add butter to the pot. In a small bowl, whisk together cream and cornstarch until smooth, then whisk mixture into the pot and add remaining 1 teaspoon Cajun seasoning. Continue sautéing 5 minutes to allow it to thicken. To serve, place a spoonful of sauce on a plate, then place a fillet on top of sauce. Top with an additional spoonful of sauce. Serve warm.

PER SERVING:

CALORIES: 274 | FAT: 18g | SODIUM: 673mg | CARBOHYDRATES: 3g | FIBER: 0g | SUGAR: 0g | PROTEIN: 22g

Creamy Tuscan Salmon

This recipe is loaded with creamy, mouthwatering flavor and gives you a plate that you'll want to lick clean thanks to all that savory sauce. This salmon feels like a fancy entrée, but it comes together in just minutes right in your kitchen.

Hands-On Time: 5 minutes
Cook Time: 8 minutes 30 seconds

Serves 4

2 tablespoons olive oil
1 tablespoon salted butter
4 cloves garlic, peeled and minced
1 cup halved grape tomatoes
1 cup chopped spinach
1 cup seafood stock
4 (6-ounce) salmon fillets
½ teaspoon garlic powder
¼ teaspoon dried oregano
¼ teaspoon dried rosemary
¼ teaspoon crushed red pepper
1 tablespoon grated lemon zest
3 tablespoons lemon juice
2 tablespoons heavy whipping cream

1 Press the Sauté button on an Instant Pot® and allow to heat until the display reads "Hot." Add olive oil, butter, and garlic to the pot. Sauté 30 seconds, then add tomatoes, spinach, and stock. Press the Cancel button.

2 Add fillets to the Instant Pot® and sprinkle with garlic powder, oregano, rosemary, crushed red pepper, lemon zest, and lemon juice. Place the lid on the Instant Pot® and click into place to close. Press the Pressure Cook button and adjust the timer to 3 minutes. When the timer beeps, quick-release the pressure until float valve drops. Unlock lid. When done, salmon will flake easily and have an internal temperature of at least 145°F.

3 Press the Cancel button, then the Sauté button. Stir in cream and allow sauce to thicken 5 minutes, then serve warm.

PER SERVING:

CALORIES: 432 | **FAT**: 29g | **SODIUM**: 212mg | **CARBOHYDRATES**: 4g | **FIBER**: 1g | **SUGAR**: 1g | **PROTEIN**: 34g

Seafood Stock

Seafood stock can sometimes be difficult to find in the store. The Instant Pot® makes it very easy to make your own, and it's a great way to use up the shells from your shrimp. You can use this stock to make soup or as a base in your Instant Pot® fish recipes.

Hands-On Time: 5 minutes
Cook Time: 30 minutes

Serves 6

3 pounds shrimp shells
2 large stalks celery, trimmed and chopped
1 large carrot, peeled and chopped
1 medium yellow onion, peeled and chopped
6 cups water
5 cloves garlic, peeled

FISH SCRAPS

Leftover fish scraps such as heads or bones can also be added to this stock. Doing so adds more flavor to the stock and helps to get the most use out of your food.

1 Place all ingredients in an Instant Pot®. Place the lid on the Instant Pot® and click into place to close.

2 Press the Pressure Cook button and adjust the timer to 30 minutes. When the timer beeps, allow a full natural release of pressure until float valve drops. Unlock lid.

3 Strain stock with a fine-mesh strainer and discard vegetables and shells. Store stock in a covered glass bowl or jar in the refrigerator for up to 3 days for best freshness.

PER SERVING:

CALORIES: 17 | **FAT**: 0g | **SODIUM**: 130mg | **CARBOHYDRATES**: 1g | **FIBER**: 0g | **SUGAR**: 0g | **PROTEIN**: 3g

Crab-Stuffed Peppers

Crab and bell peppers go together so well. If you're a fan of spice, try adding pickled jalapeño pepper slices on top. They'll pair great with the sweetness from the crab. You can brown the tops by placing the peppers in an oven-safe dish, uncovered, and broiling 2 minutes.

Hands-On Time: 10 minutes
Cook Time: 5 minutes

Serves 4

- 1 (6-ounce) can lump crabmeat
- ⅓ cup Italian-style bread crumbs
- 1 stalk celery, trimmed and diced
- 2 scallions, trimmed and sliced
- ½ teaspoon Old Bay Seasoning
- ½ teaspoon salt
- ¼ teaspoon ground black pepper
- 4 medium red bell peppers, tops removed and seeded
- 1 cup water

1 In a large bowl, mix crabmeat, bread crumbs, celery, scallions, Old Bay Seasoning, salt, and black pepper until well combined. Scoop one-quarter of mixture into each bell pepper and wrap each in aluminum foil.

2 Pour water into an Instant Pot® and place a steamer basket in the pot, then place peppers in basket. Place the lid on the Instant Pot® and click into place to close.

3 Press the Pressure Cook button and adjust the timer to 5 minutes. When the timer beeps, quick-release the pressure until float valve drops. Unlock lid. When done, peppers should be fork-tender. Serve warm.

PER SERVING:

CALORIES: 114 | FAT: 1g | SODIUM: 747mg | CARBOHYDRATES: 15g | FIBER: 3g | SUGAR: 6g | PROTEIN: 10g

Tomato Steamed Halibut

Halibut is a mild-flavored white fish that pairs wonderfully with fresh tomatoes. Whether you regularly enjoy halibut or are interested in learning to cook it for the first time, this recipe is a good choice.

Hands-On Time: 5 minutes
Cook Time: 3 minutes 30 seconds

Serves 4

1 tablespoon olive oil
3 cloves garlic, peeled and finely minced
1 tablespoon salted butter
2 cups grape tomatoes
2 tablespoons chopped capers
1 cup water
4 (4-ounce) halibut fillets
½ teaspoon salt
¼ teaspoon ground black pepper
1 medium lemon, sliced
2 fresh basil leaves, sliced

WHAT ARE CAPERS?

Capers are buds from the caper bush. They have a briny but lightly citrusy flavor and are popular in Mediterranean-style dishes. They come in jars and are often found near pickles in grocery stores.

1 Press the Sauté button on an Instant Pot® and allow to heat until the display reads "Hot." Add olive oil and garlic. Sauté 30 seconds, then add butter and tomatoes. Press the Cancel button. Sprinkle capers into the pot and pour in water.

2 Place fillets on top of tomatoes and sprinkle with salt and pepper. Place 1 lemon slice on each fillet. Place the lid on the Instant Pot® and click into place to close.

3 Press the Pressure Cook button and adjust the timer to 3 minutes. When the timer beeps, quick-release the pressure until float valve drops. Unlock lid. When done, fish will flake easily and have an internal temperature of at least 145°F. Serve each fillet on a bed of tomatoes and top with basil.

PER SERVING:

CALORIES: 175 | **FAT:** 7g | **SODIUM:** 494mg | **CARBOHYDRATES:** 4g | **FIBER:** 1g | **SUGAR:** 2g | **PROTEIN:** 22g

Vegetarian Main Dishes

The Instant Pot® truly has no limits. Whether your eating plan is completely vegetarian or you're just introducing Meatless Mondays to your family's dinner routine, this chapter has just what you need. With your Instant Pot®, you can quickly prepare satisfying, meatless, vegetable-based meals in no time. With tasty recipes such as Black Bean Burgers and Creamy Portobello Risotto, this chapter will keep you inspired to explore a wide variety of meatless options.

Spaghetti Squash 174

Three-Bean Chili 175

Butternut Squash Chili 177

Chickpea Curry 178

Vegetable Dumplings 179

Pierogis 180

Creamy Portobello Risotto 181

Italian Zucchini 182

Ravioli Lasagna 184

Black Bean Burgers 185

Kale and Goat Cheese–Stuffed Portobellos 186

Quinoa and Sweet Potato Bowl 187

Vegetable Lo Mein 189

Barbecue Lentil Sandwiches 190

Bean and Rice Burritos 191

Baked Sweet Potatoes 192

Spaghetti Squash

Spaghetti squash is a great low-carb option to replace noodles, but it can take almost an hour to roast. Pressure cooking makes it easier than ever to get those delicious strands separated and ready to eat. Spaghetti squash strands are soft and thin, similar to angel-hair pasta. But the taste is not similar; this squash has a nutty and mild taste with a hint of sweetness. Feel free to add your favorite pasta sauce to this recipe.

Hands-On Time: 5 minutes
Cook Time: 8 minutes

Serves 4

1 cup water
1 (4-pound) spaghetti
   squash, halved lengthwise
   and seeded
2 tablespoons salted butter
1 teaspoon Italian seasoning
½ teaspoon salt
¼ teaspoon ground black
   pepper

1 Pour water into an Instant Pot® and place the trivet in the pot®, then place squash on trivet, with cut side facing up. Place the lid on the Instant Pot® and click into place to close.

2 Press the Pressure Cook button and adjust the timer to 8 minutes. When the timer beeps, quick-release the pressure until float valve drops. Unlock lid.

3 Carefully transfer squash to a clean work surface and let cool for 5 minutes. Use a fork to scrape strands from the shells and place in a large bowl. Toss with butter, Italian seasoning, salt, and pepper. Serve warm.

PER SERVING:

CALORIES: 103 | **FAT:** 6g | **SODIUM:** 370mg | **CARBOHYDRATES:** 13g | **FIBER:** 3g | **SUGAR:** 5g | **PROTEIN:** 1g

Three-Bean Chili

Whether you don't eat meat or just enjoy the occasional meat-free meal, this chili can be a great alternative to the typical beef chili. It's just as filling and loaded with protein and fiber. Each type of bean adds its own unique texture to this dish.

Hands-On Time: 10 minutes
Cook Time: 12 minutes

Serves 8

2 tablespoons olive oil
1 large yellow onion, peeled and diced
2 large green bell peppers, seeded and diced
1 large carrot, peeled and chopped
2 tablespoons tomato paste
1½ tablespoons chili powder
1 teaspoon ground cumin
1 teaspoon garlic powder
½ teaspoon salt
1 (14.5-ounce) can diced tomatoes
1 (16-ounce) can kidney beans, drained and rinsed
1 (15-ounce) can black beans, drained and rinsed
1 (16-ounce) can pinto beans, drained and rinsed
2 cups vegetable broth

1 Press the Sauté button on an Instant Pot® and allow to heat until the display reads "Hot." Add olive oil, onion, bell peppers, and carrot. Sauté 3 minutes until vegetables begin to soften. Add tomato paste, chili powder, cumin, garlic powder, and salt. Sauté 1 additional minute.

2 Press the Cancel button. Pour tomatoes into the pot, then add kidney beans, black beans, pinto beans, and broth. Stir.

3 Place the lid on the Instant Pot® and click into place to close. Press the Pressure Cook button and adjust the timer to 8 minutes. When the timer beeps, quick-release the pressure until float valve drops. Unlock lid. When done, chili will be thick and beans will be soft. Serve warm.

PER SERVING:

CALORIES: 206 | FAT: 4g | SODIUM: 790mg | CARBOHYDRATES: 33g | FIBER: 9g | SUGAR: 5g | PROTEIN: 10g

Butternut Squash Chili

For a unique twist on traditional beef chili, this butternut squash recipe is a delicious alternative. The natural sweetness pairs well with the smoky chipotle flavor that you're sure to love.

Hands-On Time: 15 minutes
Cook Time: 7 minutes 30 seconds

Serves 5

2 tablespoons olive oil
1 large yellow onion, peeled and diced
1 medium green bell pepper, seeded and diced
1 medium red bell pepper, seeded and diced
1 large carrot, peeled and diced
1 cup sliced cremini mushrooms
1 tablespoon chili powder
2 teaspoons chipotle powder
1 teaspoon ground cumin
1 (3-pound) butternut squash, peeled and cut into ½" cubes
1 (14.5-ounce) can diced tomatoes
1 tablespoon tomato paste
2 cups vegetable broth
2 (15-ounce) cans black beans, drained and rinsed

1 Press the Sauté button on an Instant Pot® and allow to heat until the display reads "Hot." Add olive oil, onion, bell peppers, carrot, and mushrooms. Sauté 3 minutes until vegetables begin to soften. Press the Cancel button.

2 Add chili powder, chipotle powder, and cumin. Sauté 30 seconds, then add squash, tomatoes, tomato paste, broth, and black beans. Stir until well combined. Place the lid on the Instant Pot® and click into place to close.

3 Press the Pressure Cook button and adjust the timer to 4 minutes. When the timer beeps, quick-release the pressure until float valve drops. Unlock lid. Serve warm.

PER SERVING:

CALORIES: 303 | FAT: 6g | SODIUM: 1,002mg | CARBOHYDRATES: 51g | FIBER: 19g | SUGAR: 9g | PROTEIN: 13g

Chickpea Curry

Chickpeas are an excellent source of fiber, and they work nicely with a wide variety of flavors. Curry is a flavorful sauce dish full of warm spices. Chickpeas can withstand quite a bit of cooking before becoming overly soft; they add a texture similar to potato cubes. Try this dish alongside flatbread and a serving of steamed rice.

Hands-On Time: 10 minutes
Cook Time: 9 minutes

Serves 6

- 2 tablespoons refined coconut oil
- ½ medium yellow onion, peeled and chopped
- 1 clove garlic, peeled and finely minced
- 1 tablespoon tomato paste
- 1 teaspoon garam masala
- 1 teaspoon curry powder
- ½ teaspoon salt
- ¼ teaspoon ground black pepper
- 1 (14.5-ounce) can diced tomatoes
- 1 cup vegetable stock
- 2 (15-ounce) cans chickpeas, drained and rinsed
- 1 (13-ounce) can full-fat coconut milk

1. Press the Sauté button on an Instant Pot® and allow to heat until the display reads "Hot." Add coconut oil and onion to the pot. Sauté 2 minutes until onion softens. Add garlic, tomato paste, garam masala, curry powder, salt, and pepper to the pot. Sauté 2 minutes until fragrant.

2. Press the Cancel button. Pour diced tomatoes into the pot and use a wooden spoon to scrape any browned bits off the bottom. Pour in stock and chickpeas. Place the lid on the Instant Pot® and click into place to close. Press the Pressure Cook button and adjust the timer to 5 minutes. When the timer beeps, quick-release the pressure until float valve drops. Unlock lid.

3. Stir in coconut milk until well combined and creamy. Serve warm.

PER SERVING:

CALORIES: 310 | **FAT**: 18g | **SODIUM**: 679mg | **CARBOHYDRATES**: 28g | **FIBER**: 7g | **SUGAR**: 6g | **PROTEIN**: 9g

Vegetable Dumplings

These dumplings are full of healthy vegetables and lots of flavor. They're steamed to perfection and ready to eat in less than 20 minutes.

Hands-On Time: 10 minutes
Cook Time: 7 minutes 30 seconds

Serves 4

1 tablespoon coconut oil

2 cups napa cabbage, finely shredded

1 large carrot, peeled and finely shredded

4 ounces cremini mushrooms, thinly sliced

1 tablespoon grated ginger

2 tablespoons low-sodium soy sauce

1 large egg

½ teaspoon salt

2 teaspoons sesame oil

1 teaspoon rice wine vinegar

16 wonton wrappers

1½ cups water, plus more for brushing wrappers

1   Press the Sauté button on an Instant Pot® and allow to heat until the display reads "Hot." Add coconut oil, cabbage, carrot, and mushrooms. Sauté 5 minutes until vegetables soften. Add ginger and cook 30 seconds, then press the Cancel button. Transfer vegetables to a large bowl and rinse out the Instant Pot®, then wipe it dry.

2   Let vegetables cool 5 minutes, then whisk in soy sauce, egg, salt, sesame oil, and vinegar. Lay wonton wrappers out flat on a clean work surface. Place 1 tablespoon filling on 1 wonton wrapper. Using your hands or a small pastry brush, brush water around the edges of the wrapper, then fold in half and press the edges to seal. Repeat with remaining ingredients.

3   Pour water into the Instant Pot®. Spray a steamer basket with nonstick cooking spray. Place dumplings in prepared basket in a single layer. Two-tiered steamer trays will also work if needed. Place basket in the pot. Place the lid on the Instant Pot® and click into place to close. Press the Pressure Cook button and adjust the timer to 2 minutes. When the timer beeps, quick-release the pressure until float valve drops. Unlock lid. When done, dumplings should be soft. Serve warm.

PER SERVING:

CALORIES: 189 | FAT: 7g | SODIUM: 729mg | CARBOHYDRATES: 25g | FIBER: 2g | SUGAR: 3g | PROTEIN: 7g

Pierogis

Pierogis are dumplings filled with soft potatoes. They are budget friendly and cook in just minutes. Keep a bag on hand for when you need a quick meal and don't have much time. Rather than boiling water or sautéing, you can simply turn on the Instant Pot® and come back to a tasty meal that's bursting with delicious, cheesy goodness. Browning them after the initial cooking adds a nice crunch to the dish, but feel free to omit if you prefer steamed only.

Hands-On Time: 5 minutes
Cook Time: 10 minutes

Serves 4

1 (1-pound) bag frozen Cheddar and potato pierogis
1 cup water
2 tablespoons salted butter
2 teaspoons olive oil

1 Place pierogis in a steamer basket. Pour water into an Instant Pot® and place the steamer basket in the pot.

2 Place the lid on the Instant Pot® and click into place to close. Press the Pressure Cook button and adjust the timer to 4 minutes. When the timer beeps, quick-release the pressure until float valve drops. Unlock lid.

3 Press the Cancel button. Remove basket and pierogis and set aside. Pour water out of the pot and wipe completely dry. Press the Sauté button on the Instant Pot® and allow to heat until the display reads "Hot." Add butter and olive oil to the pot. Add steamed pierogis and sauté until golden brown on both sides, about 6 minutes. Serve warm.

PER SERVING:

CALORIES: 242 | **FAT:** 10g | **SODIUM:** 537mg | **CARBOHYDRATES:** 31g | **FIBER:** 1g | **SUGAR:** 1g | **PROTEIN:** 5g

Creamy Portobello Risotto

Portobellos have a distinct earthiness that brings dishes together and makes things taste so good. This creamy dish adds vegetables to a classic risotto for a savory meal that you'll love.

Hands-On Time: 5 minutes
Cook Time: 9 minutes 30 seconds

Serves 4

- 4 tablespoons salted butter
- 1 medium yellow onion, peeled and finely diced
- 8 ounces portobello mushrooms, thinly sliced
- 2 cloves garlic, peeled and finely minced
- 1½ cups Arborio rice
- ½ cup green peas
- 3 cups vegetable broth
- ½ teaspoon salt
- ¼ teaspoon ground black pepper
- ½ cup grated Parmesan cheese

1   Press the Sauté button on an Instant Pot® and allow to heat until the display reads "Hot." Add butter, onion, and mushrooms to the pot. Sauté 3 minutes until vegetables begin to soften. Add garlic and rice to the pot and sauté 30 seconds. Press the Cancel button.

2   Add peas, broth, salt, and pepper. Place the lid on the Instant Pot® and click into place to close. Press the Pressure Cook button and adjust the timer to 6 minutes. When the timer beeps, quick-release the pressure until float valve drops. Unlock lid.

3   Use a rubber spatula to stir in Parmesan until fully combined. Serve warm.

PER SERVING:

CALORIES: 470 | FAT: 14g | SODIUM: 1,215mg | CARBOHYDRATES: 71g | FIBER: 4g | SUGAR: 5g | PROTEIN: 11g

Italian Zucchini

Zucchini goes amazingly well with tomato sauce. Zucchini has a natural sweetness that comes out when it cooks, complementing the acidity in tomato sauce. This dish is simple, but you'll be impressed with how delicious it is with just a handful of ingredients.

Hands-On Time: 10 minutes
Cook Time: 2 minutes

Serves 4

- ½ cup marinara sauce
- ½ cup water
- 1 tablespoon tomato paste
- 2 teaspoons Italian seasoning
- ½ teaspoon salt
- 4 medium zucchini, ends trimmed, quartered lengthwise and cut into ½" thickness
- 1 cup shredded mozzarella cheese
- ¼ cup grated Parmesan cheese
- 2 basil leaves, sliced
- ¼ teaspoon crushed red pepper

1 Place marinara sauce, water, tomato paste, Italian seasoning, and salt in an Instant Pot® and stir to combine. Add zucchini to the pot.

2 Place the lid on the Instant Pot® and click into place to close. Press the Pressure Cook button and adjust the timer to 2 minutes. When the timer beeps, quick-release the pressure until float valve drops. Unlock lid.

3 Sprinkle mozzarella and Parmesan over top. Allow 5 minutes for cheese to melt from the residual heat. Top with basil and crushed red pepper, then serve.

PER SERVING:

CALORIES: 144 | FAT: 6g | SODIUM: 735mg | CARBOHYDRATES: 12g | FIBER: 3g | SUGAR: 8g | PROTEIN: 10g

Ravioli Lasagna

This meal is an excellent go-to for the weekend. It features the flavors of lasagna but uses frozen ravioli as the layers so there's no fussing with long noodles or boiling. It's easy to keep a bag of frozen ravioli in the freezer so you can quickly whip up this meal when the time is right. If you want to brown the cheese on top, broil in the oven 5 minutes at the end.

Hands-On Time: 10 minutes
Cook Time: 40 minutes

Serves 4

1 cup marinara sauce
15 frozen cheese ravioli
1 cup shredded mozzarella cheese
½ cup grated Parmesan cheese
½ cup full-fat ricotta cheese
¼ teaspoon salt
⅛ teaspoon ground black pepper
1 teaspoon Italian seasoning
1 cup water

1 Spray a 6" round baking pan with nonstick cooking spray. Pour ¼ cup marinara sauce into prepared pan, then place a layer of 5 ravioli on top. Place ¼ cup mozzarella and sprinkle 1 tablespoon Parmesan on top. In a small bowl, mix ricotta, salt, pepper, and Italian seasoning. Scatter 2 tablespoons ricotta mixture on top of Parmesan.

2 Continue the next two layers in the same order, with remaining ¼ cup mozzarella on top. Cover pan tightly with aluminum foil. Pour water into an Instant Pot® and place the trivet in the pot, then place pan on trivet. Place the lid on the Instant Pot® and click into place to close.

3 Press the Pressure Cook button and adjust the timer to 40 minutes. When the timer beeps, quick-release the pressure until float valve drops. Unlock lid. The lasagna should be soft, with all cheese melted. Serve warm.

PER SERVING:

CALORIES: 390 | **FAT:** 15g | **SODIUM:** 914mg | **CARBOHYDRATES:** 39g | **FIBER:** 2g | **SUGAR:** 4g | **PROTEIN:** 21g

Black Bean Burgers

These burgers are loaded with vitamins and other nutrients. Black beans are generally firmer than other beans, making them an excellent choice for burgers. They are flavorful and hold their shape well. These burgers are topped with a fresh guacamole that balances the creamy, hearty burgers.

Hands-On Time: 10 minutes
Cook Time: 5 minutes

Serves 4

- 1 (15-ounce) can black beans, drained and rinsed
- 1 large egg
- 1 teaspoon chili powder
- ½ teaspoon ground cumin
- ¼ teaspoon garlic powder
- ½ teaspoon salt
- ½ medium red bell pepper, seeded and finely chopped
- ¼ cup canned corn, drained and rinsed
- ½ cup Italian-style bread crumbs
- 1 cup water
- 1 medium avocado, peeled, pitted, and sliced
- 2 tablespoons diced red onion
- 1 tablespoon lime juice
- 1 tablespoon chopped cilantro
- 4 burger buns

1 In a large bowl, mash beans until smooth. Mix in egg, chili powder, cumin, garlic powder, salt, bell pepper, and corn until well combined. Fold in bread crumbs until well combined. Form mixture into four equal patties.

2 Pour water into an Instant Pot® and place a steamer basket in the pot, then place patties in basket. Place the lid on the Instant Pot® and click into place to close. Press the Pressure Cook button and adjust the timer to 5 minutes. When the timer beeps, quick-release the pressure until float valve drops. Unlock lid.

3 In a small bowl, mash avocado, then fold in onion, lime juice, and cilantro. Place each burger on a bun and top with guacamole to serve.

PER SERVING:

CALORIES: 362 | **FAT:** 8g | **SODIUM:** 998mg | **CARBOHYDRATES:** 56g | **FIBER:** 12g | **SUGAR:** 5g | **PROTEIN:** 15g

Kale and Goat Cheese–Stuffed Portobellos

Portobellos are great mushrooms for stuffing. They're thick, textured, and big enough to fill with delicious ingredients. Each bite of these mushrooms is filled with three kinds of cheese. If you like a little spice, add a sprinkle of crushed red pepper. For a browned top, place mushrooms on a foil-lined baking sheet and broil in the oven 3 minutes.

Hands-On Time: 5 minutes
Cook Time: 10 minutes

Serves 4

2 ounces cream cheese, softened
½ cup crumbled goat cheese
¼ cup grated Parmesan cheese
½ teaspoon salt
⅓ cup Italian-style bread crumbs
1 cup chopped kale
4 (4") portobello mushrooms, stems removed
1 cup water

1 In a medium bowl, mix cream cheese, goat cheese, Parmesan, salt, bread crumbs, and kale until well combined.

2 Divide mixture into four even portions and spoon into each mushroom cap, pressing down to pack in filling. Pour water into an Instant Pot® and place a steamer basket in the pot, then place mushrooms in basket. Place the lid on the Instant Pot® and click into place to close.

3 Press the Pressure Cook button and adjust the timer to 10 minutes. When the timer beeps, quick-release the pressure until float valve drops. Unlock lid. When done, mushrooms will be tender and cheese will be melted. Serve warm.

PER SERVING:

CALORIES: 184 | **FAT**: 10g | **SODIUM**: 656mg | **CARBOHYDRATES**: 12g | **FIBER**: 2g | **SUGAR**: 3g | **PROTEIN**: 9g

Quinoa and Sweet Potato Bowl

The Instant Pot® is deep, which gives you the option to cook things with similar cook times together. This bowl meal cuts down on excess pans and puts the grain and potatoes together for a delicious, steamed meal in one pot. Whether you like to meticulously build your bowl and keep ingredients separate or mix it all up and enjoy, this recipe is sure to be a new favorite.

Hands-On Time: 10 minutes
Cook Time: 7 minutes

Serves 4

1 cup quinoa
1½ cups vegetable broth
1 teaspoon salt, divided
¼ teaspoon ground black pepper
2 medium sweet potatoes, peeled and cut into 1" cubes
1 (15-ounce) can chickpeas, drained and rinsed
½ teaspoon ground cumin
½ teaspoon chili powder
¼ teaspoon paprika
2 cups chopped kale
1 medium red bell pepper, seeded and sliced into ½"-thick slices
½ medium red onion, peeled and sliced

PACKED WITH PROTEIN

Quinoa has more protein than rice, making it a great alternative when you want to change things up. It also has fiber, which is important for helping you feel full.

1 Place quinoa in an Instant Pot® and pour in broth. Sprinkle with ½ teaspoon salt and black pepper. Place a steamer basket over quinoa and place sweet potatoes and chickpeas in basket. Sprinkle with cumin, chili powder, and paprika. Place the lid on the Instant Pot® and click into place to close. Press the Pressure Cook button and adjust the timer to 3 minutes. When the timer beeps, let the pressure release naturally for 10 minutes, then quick-release any remaining pressure until float valve drops. Unlock lid.

2 Remove steamer basket and fluff quinoa with a fork, then place in a large serving bowl. Top with sweet potatoes and chickpeas. Press the Cancel button. Pour any liquid from the pot and wipe dry.

3 Press the Sauté button on the Instant Pot® and allow to heat until the display reads "Hot." Put in kale, bell pepper, and onion. Sauté 4 minutes until kale wilts and bell pepper begins to soften. Scatter mixture over potatoes and chickpeas. Serve warm.

PER SERVING:

CALORIES: 329 | **FAT:** 4g | **SODIUM:** 1,058mg | **CARBOHYDRATES:** 61g | **FIBER:** 11g | **SUGAR:** 10g | **PROTEIN:** 13g

Vegetable Lo Mein

This quick noodle bowl is loaded with vegetables and flavor. It makes a great lunch because it's light and full of nutrients. The noodles are coated in an appetizing sauce that you'll come back to time and time again. Feel free to add extra vegetables or your own favorites, such as snap peas.

Hands-On Time: 5 minutes
Cook Time: 3 minutes

Serves 6

4 cups vegetable broth

1 tablespoon low-sodium soy sauce

½ teaspoon ground ginger

½ teaspoon garlic powder

¼ teaspoon onion powder

4 ounces sliced button mushrooms

1 large carrot, peeled and thinly sliced

1 medium head bok choy, trimmed

7 ounces lo mein noodles

2 scallions, trimmed and sliced

1 tablespoon toasted sesame seeds

1   Pour broth and soy sauce into an Instant Pot®, then add ginger, garlic powder, onion powder, mushrooms, carrot, and bok choy. Fan lo mein noodles out on top of vegetables and gently press down to submerge in broth.

2   Place the lid on the Instant Pot® and click into place to close. Press the Pressure Cook button and adjust the timer to 3 minutes.

3   When the timer beeps, quick-release the pressure until float valve drops. Unlock lid. Stir noodles. Serve topped with scallions and sesame seeds.

PER SERVING:

CALORIES: 159 | FAT: 2g | SODIUM: 942mg | CARBOHYDRATES: 32g | FIBER: 3g | SUGAR: 5g | PROTEIN: 7g

Barbecue Lentil Sandwiches

If you've never had lentils, this recipe is a great place to try them. Lentils are a legume and are full of fiber and nutrients. This recipe cooks them into a creamy sauce, similar to a sloppy joe in texture. The lentils are tender but not mushy.

Hands-On Time: 5 minutes
Cook Time: 16 minutes

Serves 6

1 cup brown lentils
3 cups water
$\frac{1}{2}$ teaspoon salt
$\frac{1}{4}$ teaspoon ground black pepper
$\frac{1}{2}$ teaspoon cumin
$\frac{1}{4}$ teaspoon chili powder
$\frac{1}{4}$ teaspoon onion powder
$\frac{1}{2}$ cup ketchup
2 teaspoons molasses
2 tablespoons light brown sugar, packed
1 teaspoon coconut aminos
$\frac{1}{8}$ teaspoon liquid smoke
6 burger buns

1 Place lentils in an Instant Pot® and pour in water. Sprinkle with salt, pepper, cumin, chili powder, and onion powder. Place the lid on the Instant Pot® and click into place to close. Press the Pressure Cook button and adjust the timer to 10 minutes.

2 When the timer beeps, let the pressure release naturally for 15 minutes, then quick-release any remaining pressure until float valve drops. Unlock lid. Pour lentils into a colander over a bowl, then set aside.

3 Pour out any excess liquid and wipe the pot dry with a paper towel. Press the Cancel button, then the Sauté button. Pour in ketchup, molasses, brown sugar, coconut aminos, and liquid smoke. Whisk until a sauce forms, about 1 minute. Pour lentils back into the pot and use a rubber spatula to coat lentils in sauce. Continue cooking 5 minutes until sauce is thick and lentils are well covered. Place $\frac{1}{2}$ cup lentils on each bun. Serve warm.

PER SERVING:

CALORIES: 275 | FAT: 2g | SODIUM: 611mg | CARBOHYDRATES: 54g | FIBER: 5g | SUGAR: 14g | PROTEIN: 12g

Bean and Rice Burritos

Beans and rice are a powerful combination. Not only do they taste great, but together they make a complete protein, meaning they contain all nine essential amino acids. This recipe is great for meal prep because you can make the filling and grab some whenever you need a quick meal. You can dress the burrito up as much or as little as you'd like by adding your favorite fillings such as fresh tomatoes, lettuce, jalapeños, or even warm queso.

Hands-On Time: 5 minutes
Cook Time: 3 minutes

Serves 6

1½ cups vegetable broth
1 cup long-grain white rice, rinsed and drained
1 (16-ounce) can pinto beans, drained and rinsed
½ cup canned corn, drained
1 (10-ounce) can diced tomatoes and green chiles, drained
1 cup chunky salsa
1 (1-ounce) packet taco seasoning
6 (10") flour tortillas, warmed
1½ cups shredded Mexican cheese blend
6 tablespoons sour cream
6 tablespoons guacamole

1 Pour broth into an Instant Pot®, then add rice, beans, corn, diced tomatoes and green chiles, salsa, and taco seasoning. Stir to combine. Place the lid on the Instant Pot® and click into place to close. Press the Pressure Cook button and adjust the timer to 3 minutes.

2 When the timer beeps, let the pressure release naturally for 10 minutes, then quick-release any remaining pressure until float valve drops. Unlock lid. Use a fork to fluff rice and mix filling.

3 Place tortillas on a clean work surface. Place 1 cup filling on each tortilla. Top each with ¼ cup shredded cheese, 1 tablespoon sour cream, and 1 tablespoon guacamole. Fold the left and right sides of each tortilla one-third of the way toward the center, then roll burrito away from you until closed. Serve warm.

PER SERVING:

CALORIES: 581 | FAT: 17g | SODIUM: 1,796mg | CARBOHYDRATES: 83g | FIBER: 5g | SUGAR: 8g | PROTEIN: 19g

Baked Sweet Potatoes

Sweet potatoes make a delicious and filling meal. When cooked in the Instant Pot®, they get steamed to a smooth and fluffy texture. If you aren't a fan of cinnamon, try adding a sprinkle of chipotle powder for some heat or even topping with beans and corn for a loaded potato.

Hands-On Time: 5 minutes
Cook Time: 30 minutes

Serves 4

4 medium (3") sweet potatoes
1 cup water
2 tablespoons salted butter, melted
½ teaspoon ground cinnamon

1 Use a fork to poke potatoes seven times to allow steam venting. Pour water into an Instant Pot® and place the trivet in the pot, then place potatoes on trivet.

2 Place the lid on the Instant Pot® and click into place to close. Press the Pressure Cook button and adjust the timer to 30 minutes. When the timer beeps, let the pressure release naturally for 10 minutes, then quick release any remaining pressure until float valve drops. Unlock lid.

3 When done, potatoes should be tender; a fork inserted into the center should easily pierce each potato. To serve, slice each potato in half, drizzle with butter, and sprinkle with cinnamon. Serve warm.

PER SERVING:

CALORIES: 163 | **FAT:** 5g | **SODIUM:** 117mg | **CARBOHYDRATES:** 26g | **FIBER:** 4g | **SUGAR:** 5g | **PROTEIN:** 2g

Desserts

This chapter is for the chocoholics and anyone with a sweet tooth who knows what they seek in a good dessert and likes to have homemade treats without too much work. The Instant Pot® aims to please by quickly cooking a wide variety of indulgent goodies that are sure to hit the spot whenever your cravings strike. Instant Pot® desserts are often denser than their oven-baked counterparts. Since there's not evaporation as there is in an oven, you'll find that the texture differs, and with desserts like brownies, you get gooey, fudge-like results. From Fudge Brownies to Caramel Flan, this chapter's recipes showcase satisfying desserts.

Pudding Cake 194

Crustless Vanilla Cheesecake 196

Vanilla Pound Cake 197

Stewed Apples 198

Protein-Packed Baked Apples 199

Cinnamon Apple Upside-Down Cake 201

Caramel Apple Cider 202

Slow Cooker Hot Chocolate 203

Bread Pudding 204

Banana Bread 205

Chocolate Chip Cookie Cake 206

Caramel Flan 208

Strawberry Jam 209

Slow Cooker Candied Pecans 210

Slow Cooker Chocolate Peanut Clusters 211

Fudge Brownies 213

Cinnamon Dulce de Leche 214

Rice Pudding 215

Apple Butter 216

Pudding Cake

This recipe upgrades your regular boxed cake mix. With only a few added ingredients, this recipe takes boxed cake to the next level to make it taste like something you might find in a bakery. This ultra-moist cake is full of vanilla flavor. Serve with whipped cream and fresh strawberries for an extra something special.

Hands-On Time: 10 minutes
Cook Time: 40 minutes

Serves 16

1 cup whole milk
½ cup salted butter, melted
4 large eggs
2 teaspoons vanilla extract
1 (15-ounce) box vanilla cake mix
1 (4.6-ounce) box vanilla pudding mix (not instant pudding mix)
1 cup water

FROSTING

You can serve this cake with whipped cream and fresh strawberries, your favorite glaze, or store-bought frosting. For a store-bought frosting drizzle, simply transfer frosting to a microwave-safe bowl, microwave 15 seconds, and stir. The frosting will be pourable and drizzle easily from a spoon when it's ready. You can then pour over the top of the cake, allowing it to flow down the sides. If it isn't pourable after 15 seconds, microwave in 5-second intervals, being careful not to overheat it.

1 Spray a 7-cup Bundt pan with nonstick cooking spray. In a large bowl, whisk together milk, butter, eggs, vanilla, cake mix, and pudding mix until smooth. Pour batter in prepared pan.

2 Cover pan tightly with aluminum foil. Pour water into an Instant Pot® and place the trivet in the pot, then place pan on trivet. Place the lid on the Instant Pot® and click into place to close. Press the Pressure Cook button and adjust the timer to 40 minutes. When the timer beeps, let the pressure release naturally for 10 minutes, then quick-release any remaining pressure until float valve drops. Unlock lid.

3 When done, cake should be firm to the touch and a toothpick inserted into the center should come out clean. Allow cake to cool 30 minutes before removing from pan and serving.

PER SERVING:

CALORIES: 222 | **FAT:** 9g | **SODIUM:** 298mg | **CARBOHYDRATES:** 30g | **FIBER:** 0g | **SUGAR:** 20g | **PROTEIN:** 3g

Crustless Vanilla Cheesecake

Making perfectly smooth and creamy cheesecake doesn't get much easier than setting the batter in your Instant Pot® and letting the device go to work. This recipe simplifies the process even more by skipping the crust to focus on that delicious vanilla filling. Do not use an electric mixer to mix in the eggs here; it will create air bubbles.

Hands-On Time: 10 minutes
Cook Time: 40 minutes

Serves 8

32 ounces cream cheese, softened
1 cup granulated sugar
¼ cup sour cream
3 large eggs, whisked
2 teaspoons vanilla extract
1 cup water

GRAHAM CRACKER CRUST

If you're a fan of crust, place 10 sheets of broken graham crackers and ⅓ cup salted butter, cubed, in a food processor. Process on low 20 seconds until a sand-like texture forms. Press this crust into the bottom of the springform pan before pouring in the cheesecake batter.

1 In a large bowl, beat cream cheese until smooth and fluffy, about 3 minutes. Add sugar and sour cream and continue to beat 1 minute. Using a rubber spatula, fold in eggs and vanilla.

2 Spray a 7" springform pan with nonstick cooking spray and line it with parchment paper. Pour batter into prepared pan and cover pan tightly with aluminum foil. Pour water into an Instant Pot® and place the trivet in the pot, then place pan on trivet.

3 Place the lid on the Instant Pot® and click into place to close. Press the Pressure Cook button and adjust the timer to 40 minutes. When the timer beeps, let the pressure release naturally, about 20 minutes, until float valve drops. Unlock lid. Place pan on a wire rack to cool 2 hours, then refrigerate at least 8 hours before serving.

PER SERVING:

CALORIES: 528 | FAT: 36g | SODIUM: 444mg | CARBOHYDRATES: 30g | FIBER: 0g | SUGAR: 29g | PROTEIN: 9g

Vanilla Pound Cake

This simple, sweet, moist, and dense cake is perfect for any occasion. Enjoy this cake with whipped cream and fresh berries or a spoonful of raspberry jam.

Hands-On Time: 10 minutes
Cook Time: 40 minutes

Serves 8

½ cup salted butter, softened
1 cup granulated sugar
2 large eggs
1 teaspoon vanilla extract
½ teaspoon almond extract
1¼ cups all-purpose flour
½ teaspoon baking powder
¼ teaspoon salt
½ cup whole milk
1 cup water

1 Spray a 7-cup Bundt pan with nonstick cooking spray. In a large bowl, mix all ingredients except water until well combined. Pour batter into prepared pan and cover pan tightly with aluminum foil.

2 Pour water into an Instant Pot® and place the trivet in the pot, then place pan on trivet. Place the lid on the Instant Pot® and click into place to close. Press the Pressure Cook button and adjust the timer to 40 minutes.

3 When the timer beeps, let the pressure release naturally for 10 minutes, then quick-release any remaining pressure until float valve drops. Unlock lid. When cake is done, a toothpick inserted into the center will come out clean. Remove pan from the Instant Pot® and let cool 10 minutes, then invert onto a large platter. Serve at room temperature or chilled.

PER SERVING:

CALORIES: 298 | **FAT:** 12g | **SODIUM:** 219mg | **CARBOHYDRATES:** 41g | **FIBER:** 1g | **SUGAR:** 26g | **PROTEIN:** 4g

Stewed Apples

These sweet and soft apples are perfect for making in the fall. Whether you enjoy a comforting bowl by themselves or on top of a scoop of ice cream, the cinnamon goodness just can't be beat. This recipe calls for Fuji apples because of their balance of sweetness and tartness, but if you have Gala or Honeycrisp apples on hand, those are excellent swaps.

Hands-On Time: 10 minutes
Cook Time: 7 minutes

Serves 6

4 large Fuji apples, peeled, cored, and cut into ½"-thick slices
1 cup apple juice
½ cup light brown sugar, lightly packed
1 tablespoon ground cinnamon
2 teaspoons cornstarch
2 tablespoons water

1 Place apples in an Instant Pot®. Add apple juice, brown sugar, and cinnamon. Place the lid on the Instant Pot® and click into place to close.

2 Press the Pressure Cook button and adjust the timer to 4 minutes. When the timer beeps, quick-release the pressure until float valve drops. Unlock lid.

3 In a small bowl, whisk together cornstarch and water. Press the Cancel button, then the Sauté button. Pour cornstarch mixture into apples and sauté 3 minutes to thicken. When done, apples will be tender. Serve warm.

PER SERVING:

CALORIES: 164 | **FAT**: 0g | **SODIUM**: 6mg | **CARBOHYDRATES**: 43g | **FIBER**: 3g | **SUGAR**: 36g | **PROTEIN**: 1g

Protein-Packed Baked Apples

This healthy dessert has tender apple in each bite. The cool and creamy yogurt adds protein to help keep you full and energized. The nuts add a bit of crunch to make this dessert check off all the boxes (with none of the guilt).

Hands-On Time: 5 minutes
Cook Time: 3 minutes

Serves 4

1 cup water
4 medium Honeycrisp apples, cored
1½ teaspoons ground cinnamon, divided
1 cup full-fat plain Greek yogurt
¼ cup chopped toasted pecans
2 teaspoons honey

1 Pour water into an Instant Pot® and place the trivet in the pot, then place apples on trivet. Sprinkle 1 teaspoon cinnamon over apples. Place the lid on the Instant Pot® and click into place to close.

2 Press the Pressure Cook button and adjust the timer to 3 minutes. When the timer beeps, let the pressure release naturally for 2 minutes, then quick-release any remaining pressure until float valve drops. Unlock lid.

3 To serve, cut each apple in half and place cut sides up in a bowl. Top with yogurt and scatter pecans over top. Sprinkle with remaining ½ teaspoon cinnamon and drizzle with honey.

PER SERVING:

CALORIES: 234 | **FAT:** 7g | **SODIUM:** 21mg | **CARBOHYDRATES:** 36g | **FIBER:** 5g | **SUGAR:** 29g | **PROTEIN:** 6g

Cinnamon Apple Upside-Down Cake

Get ready to take everything you thought you knew about cinnamon apple treats and turn it on its head. This upside-down cake is wonderfully moist and packed with warm flavors.

Hands-On Time: 10 minutes
Cook Time: 40 minutes

Serves 8

½ cup sour cream
½ cup light brown sugar, packed
2 tablespoons granulated sugar
1 large egg
½ teaspoon salt
1 teaspoon ground cinnamon
1 teaspoon vanilla extract
1½ cups all-purpose flour
1 teaspoon baking powder
1 (21-ounce) can apple pie filling
1 cup water

PEACHES

You can swap the apple pie filling in this recipe for canned peach pie filling. It's just as delicious and a great flavor to go with a spoonful of whipped cream.

1   In a large bowl, mix sour cream, brown sugar, granulated sugar, egg, salt, cinnamon, and vanilla. Whisk in flour and baking powder until a smooth batter forms.

2   Spray a 6" round baking pan with nonstick cooking spray. Pour pie filling into prepared pan. Place batter on top of pie filling. Cover pan tightly with aluminum foil.

3   Pour water into an Instant Pot® and place the trivet in the pot, then place pan on trivet. Place the lid on the Instant Pot® and click into place to close. Press the Pressure Cook button and adjust the timer to 40 minutes. When the timer beeps, let the pressure release naturally for 15 minutes, then quick-release any remaining pressure until float valve drops. Unlock lid. Serve warm.

PER SERVING:

CALORIES: 262 | **FAT:** 3g | **SODIUM:** 260mg | **CARBOHYDRATES:** 55g | **FIBER:** 2g | **SUGAR:** 27g | **PROTEIN:** 4g

Caramel Apple Cider

The Instant Pot® also excels at making delicious drinks. If you're making cider for a group, this is an easy method that will also keep the drink warm until it's time to enjoy it. This drink tastes like a warm apple juice filled with seasonal spices, which makes it as comforting as it is tasty.

Hands-On Time: 10 minutes
Cook Time: 10 minutes

Serves 4

8 cups water
¼ cup light brown sugar, packed
¼ cup granulated sugar
2 teaspoons ground cinnamon
¼ teaspoon ground nutmeg
3 large Gala apples, cored and quartered
½ medium navel orange, sliced
¼ cup caramel topping
8 tablespoons whipped cream

1 Pour water into an Instant Pot® and whisk in brown sugar, granulated sugar, cinnamon, and nutmeg until well combined. Add apple pieces and orange slices.

2 Place the lid on the Instant Pot® and click into place to close. Press the Pressure Cook button and adjust the timer to 10 minutes. When the timer beeps, quick-release the pressure until float valve drops. Unlock lid.

3 Use a potato masher or fork to mash apples into the liquid. Use a fine-mesh strainer over a large bowl to remove large chunks. To serve, drizzle a tablespoon of caramel into each cup, then fill with apple cider. Top with whipped cream and garnish with additional sprinkle of cinnamon if desired. Serve warm.

PER SERVING:

CALORIES: 203 | **FAT**: 1g | **SODIUM**: 75mg | **CARBOHYDRATES**: 50g | **FIBER**: 2g | **SUGAR**: 33g | **PROTEIN**: 1g

Slow Cooker Hot Chocolate

Hot chocolate is perfect for snowy days, but rushing to get it made when you come in is never fun. This creamy cup of hot chocolate will be ready and waiting for you. It stays warm so you can enjoy it whenever the time is right, and you can easily double it for a crowd. Try it with whipped cream, marshmallows, or both!

Hands-On Time: 5 minutes
Cook Time: 1 hour

Serves 6

4 cups whole milk
1 cup heavy whipping cream
1 cup water
½ cup unsweetened cocoa powder
⅓ cup granulated sugar
¼ cup milk chocolate chips
1 teaspoon vanilla extract
¼ teaspoon salt

1 Whisk all ingredients in an Instant Pot®. Press the Slow Cook button and adjust the timer to 1 hour. Cover with a glass slow cooker lid. Whisk occasionally.

2 When the timer beeps, allow the pot to stay on Keep Warm mode. The hot chocolate will be medium brown in color and creamy.

3 Use a ladle to scoop hot chocolate into mugs and serve warm.

PER SERVING:

CALORIES: 334 | **FAT:** 21g | **SODIUM:** 188mg | **CARBOHYDRATES:** 28g | **FIBER:** 3g | **SUGAR:** 24g | **PROTEIN:** 8g

Bread Pudding

Get ready for your new favorite way to use leftover bread. This moist and creamy Bread Pudding has a deliciously creamy custard filling and a crusty exterior. If you have some bread that's past its prime but still good, this recipe is perfect for you.

Hands-On Time: 10 minutes
Cook Time: 30 minutes

Serves 8

1 cup whole milk
1 large egg
1 large egg yolk
¼ cup chopped pecans
¼ cup granulated sugar
2 tablespoons light brown sugar, packed
1 teaspoon ground cinnamon
¼ teaspoon ground nutmeg
½ teaspoon salt
6 ounces French bread, cut into ½" cubes
1 cup water

1 Spray a 6" round cake pan with nonstick cooking spray and set aside. In a large bowl, whisk together milk, egg, egg yolk, pecans, granulated sugar, brown sugar, cinnamon, nutmeg, and salt until well combined. Gently fold in bread and toss to coat.

2 Transfer mixture to prepared pan and gently press down on bread to ensure all pieces are coated and close together. Cover pan tightly with aluminum foil.

3 Pour water into an Instant Pot® and place the trivet in the pot, then place pan on trivet. Place the lid on the Instant Pot® and click into place to close. Press the Pressure Cook button and adjust the timer to 30 minutes. When the timer beeps, quick-release the pressure until float valve drops. Unlock lid. Allow 10 minutes on the counter to cool, then invert onto a plate to slice and serve warm.

PER SERVING:

CALORIES: 153 | **FAT**: 5g | **SODIUM**: 296mg | **CARBOHYDRATES**: 23g | **FIBER**: 1g | **SUGAR**: 12g | **PROTEIN**: 5g

Banana Bread

This Banana Bread comes out perfectly moist and rich in flavor. The cinnamon paired with the sugar is blissful, and the chopped walnuts add the perfect crunch in every bite. Use very ripe bananas, with plenty of black spots on the peel, to make sure you're getting the best taste.

Hands-On Time: 10 minutes
Cook Time: 55 minutes

Serves 8

- 3 large ripe bananas, peeled and mashed
- 1 large egg
- ¼ cup salted butter, melted
- ¼ cup granulated sugar
- ¼ cup light brown sugar, packed
- ¼ teaspoon salt
- ½ teaspoon ground cinnamon
- 1 teaspoon vanilla extract
- 1 teaspoon baking soda
- 1½ cups all-purpose flour
- ¼ cup chopped walnuts
- 1 cup water

1 In a large bowl, mix bananas, egg, butter, granulated sugar, brown sugar, salt, cinnamon, vanilla, and baking soda until well combined. Mix in flour until well combined. Fold in walnuts.

2 Spray a 6" round baking pan with nonstick cooking spray and pour batter into prepared pan. Cover pan tightly with aluminum foil. Pour water into an Instant Pot® and place the trivet in the pot, then place pan on trivet.

3 Place the lid on the Instant Pot® and click into place to close. Press the Pressure Cook button and adjust the timer to 55 minutes. When the timer beeps, let the pressure release naturally for about 15 minutes, then quick-release any remaining pressure until float valve drops. Unlock lid. Remove pan from Instant Pot® and allow to cool 10 minutes before slicing. Serve warm.

PER SERVING:

CALORIES: 266 | FAT: 8g | SODIUM: 287mg | CARBOHYDRATES: 43g | FIBER: 2g | SUGAR: 19g | PROTEIN: 4g

Chocolate Chip Cookie Cake

This simple recipe will squash all your cookie cravings. With the texture of a soft and gooey cookie and all the taste you love, this irresistible treat is the perfect blend of chewy and chocolaty. Make this massive dessert even more indulgent with a heaping scoop of vanilla ice cream. If you love cookie cake, this recipe is going to be your new favorite.

Hands-On Time: 10 minutes
Cook Time: 40 minutes

Serves 6

8 tablespoons salted butter, softened
½ cup light brown sugar, packed
1 teaspoon vanilla extract
1 large egg
1 cup all-purpose flour
¼ teaspoon baking powder
½ teaspoon baking soda
½ cup semisweet chocolate chips
1 cup water

1 In a large bowl, beat butter, brown sugar, and vanilla until smooth and fluffy, about 3 minutes. Mix in egg. In a small bowl, whisk together flour, baking powder, and baking soda. Slowly add flour mixture to butter mixture and stir until well combined. Fold in chocolate chips.

2 Spray a 6" round baking pan with nonstick cooking spray and line it with parchment paper. Transfer cookie batter to prepared pan. Cover pan tightly with aluminum foil. Pour water into an Instant Pot® and place the trivet in the pot, then place pan on trivet.

3 Place the lid on the Instant Pot® and click into place to close. Press the Pressure Cook button and adjust the timer to 40 minutes. When the timer beeps, let the pressure release naturally for 10 minutes, then quick-release any remaining pressure until float valve drops. Unlock lid. A toothpick inserted into the center should come out clean. Remove pan from Instant Pot® and allow to cool 15 minutes before serving.

PER SERVING:

CALORIES: 367 | **FAT:** 19g | **SODIUM:** 265mg | **CARBOHYDRATES:** 44g | **FIBER:** 1g | **SUGAR:** 26g | **PROTEIN:** 4g

Caramel Flan

Flan is a creamy egg-based custard that is traditionally topped with a caramel sauce. This simple Instant Pot® version is made in just a fraction of the time of traditional methods. Try topping yours with a dollop of whipped cream for even more creamy goodness.

Hands-On Time: 5 minutes
Cook Time: 15 minutes

Serves 8

¼ cup caramel sauce, warmed
½ cup sweetened condensed milk
¼ cup evaporated milk
3 large egg yolks
1 teaspoon vanilla extract
4 ounces cream cheese, softened
1 cup water

1 Spray a 6" round baking pan with nonstick cooking spray. Pour warm caramel into prepared pan and swirl it to coat the pan.

2 In a large bowl, whisk sweetened condensed milk, evaporated milk, egg yolks, vanilla, and cream cheese together until smooth. Pour mixture over caramel. Tightly wrap pan in aluminum foil.

3 Pour water into an Instant Pot® place the trivet in the pot, then place pan on trivet. Place the lid on the Instant Pot® and click into place to close. Press the Pressure Cook button and adjust the timer to 15 minutes. When the timer beeps, let the pressure release naturally for 10 minutes, then quick-release any remaining pressure until float valve drops. Unlock lid. Allow flan to cool on a wire rack 5 minutes, then invert onto a plate, allowing caramel to coat the top and sides. Chill at least 6 hours before slicing and serving.

PER SERVING:

CALORIES: 168 | **FAT:** 8g | **SODIUM:** 122mg | **CARBOHYDRATES:** 19g | **FIBER:** 0g | **SUGAR:** 11g | **PROTEIN:** 4g

Strawberry Jam

Jam is perfect for filling cakes, topping ice cream, and spreading on toast. It's easy to make, and a great way to use extra strawberries. This fresh-tasting jam has a great balance of sweet and tart.

Hands-On Time: 10 minutes
Cook Time: 7 minutes

Serves 16

2 pounds strawberries, hulled
1 cup water
¾ cup granulated sugar
2 tablespoons lemon juice
2 tablespoons cornstarch

MIXED BERRY

You can make this jam into mixed berry jam by swapping 1 cup strawberries for 1 cup raspberries. It will add a nice depth of flavor. You can also use blackberries, but you'll need to use a fine-mesh strainer to remove the seeds after the cooking is completed and before the cooling.

1   Place strawberries, water, sugar, and lemon juice in an Instant Pot® and stir.

2   Place the lid on the Instant Pot® and click into place to close. Press the Pressure Cook button and adjust the timer to 2 minutes. When the timer beeps, let the pressure release naturally for 10 minutes, then quick-release any remaining pressure until float valve drops. Unlock lid.

3   Transfer 4 tablespoons liquid from the pot to a small bowl. Whisk cornstarch into the liquid, then stir mixture into the pot. Press the Cancel button, then the Sauté button. Stir and sauté to thicken 5 minutes. When done, jam will be thick and coat the back of a spoon. Allow to completely cool before serving.

PER SERVING:

CALORIES: 57 | FAT: 0g | SODIUM: 0mg | CARBOHYDRATES: 15g | FIBER: 1g | SUGAR: 12g | PROTEIN: 0g

Slow Cooker Candied Pecans

This recipe is great for a quick snack but is sweet enough for a dessert. The crunchy pecans are covered in a deliciously sweet coating. They smell delicious while cooking, which is a nice bonus.

Hands-On Time: 5 minutes
Cook Time: 3 hours

Serves 12

2 large egg whites
2 teaspoons vanilla extract
1 cup light brown sugar, packed
½ cup granulated sugar
2 teaspoons ground cinnamon
¼ teaspoon salt
3 cups whole pecans

1 In a large bowl, whisk egg whites and vanilla. Whisk in brown sugar, granulated sugar, cinnamon, and salt until well combined. Stir in pecans until well coated.

2 Spray an Instant Pot® with nonstick cooking spray. Transfer mixture to the pot. Place a glass slow cooker lid on the pot.

3 Press the Slow Cook button and adjust the timer to 3 hours. Stir mixture every 30 minutes to ensure even cooking. Pecans will feel soft while warm. Line a baking sheet with parchment paper. When the timer beeps, place pecans on prepared sheet and allow to cool 30 minutes. They will get crunchy as they cool. Store in an airtight container for up to 1 week at room temperature.

PER SERVING:

CALORIES: 278 | FAT: 17g | SODIUM: 62mg | CARBOHYDRATES: 30g | FIBER: 3g | SUGAR: 28g | PROTEIN: 3g

Slow Cooker Chocolate Peanut Clusters

These delectable peanut clusters are fast, easy, and sure to please a crowd! Even better, the Instant Pot® takes the mess out of working with melted chocolate by containing the whole recipe in just one pot. You'll be making these delicious treats all holiday season!

Hands-On Time: 5 minutes
Cook Time: 1 hour 30 minutes

Serves 20

2 cups salted Virginia peanuts
1½ cups chocolate melting wafers

GET CREATIVE!

Feel free to add your own twist on these clusters, like stirring in mini marshmallows right before scooping out, using a cup of cashews for mixed nuts, or adding a sprinkle of flaky sea salt. If making these for a crowd or gift, try a drizzle of white chocolate for a beautiful presentation.

1 Place peanuts in an Instant Pot® and place a glass slow cooker lid on the pot. Press the Slow Cook button twice to adjust the temperature to "Less." Allow peanuts to slow cook 1 hour, stirring occasionally. Remove lid.

2 Scatter chocolate wafers over top of peanuts. Replace the slow cooker lid and cook 30 minutes, stirring twice during the cook time. Chocolate will melt and coat nuts.

3 When the timer beeps, stir nuts and chocolate to ensure all peanuts are coated. Line a large baking sheet with parchment paper. Scoop about 2 tablespoons together and place in a small mound on prepared sheet. Repeat to make 20 clusters. Place in refrigerator to chill 2 hours before serving.

PER SERVING:

CALORIES: 153 | **FAT**: 11g | **SODIUM**: 56mg | **CARBOHYDRATES**: 10g | **FIBER**: 2g | **SUGAR**: 7g | **PROTEIN**: 5g

Fudge Brownies

These brownies are dense, gooey, and filled with chocolate. If you love brownie sundaes, this is your perfect base. Top it with a scoop of vanilla ice cream and a drizzle of hot fudge or chocolate sauce for the perfect brownie à la mode.

Hands-On Time: 10 minutes
Cook Time: 40 minutes

Serves 8

1 cup granulated sugar
¼ cup salted butter
2 large eggs
1 teaspoon vanilla extract
¼ cup vegetable oil
½ cup unsweetened cocoa powder
½ cup all-purpose flour
1 tablespoon cornstarch
½ cup semisweet chocolate chips
1 cup water

1 In a large bowl, whisk together sugar, butter, eggs, vanilla, and vegetable oil. Whisk in cocoa powder, flour, and cornstarch until smooth and well combined. Fold in chocolate chips.

2 Spray a 6" round baking pan with nonstick cooking spray. Transfer batter to prepared pan and cover tightly with aluminum foil. Pour water into an Instant Pot® and place the trivet in the pot, then place pan on trivet. Place the lid on the Instant Pot® and click into place to close.

3 Press the Pressure Cook button and adjust the timer to 40 minutes. When the timer beeps, let the pressure release naturally for 10 minutes, then quick-release any remaining pressure until float valve drops. Unlock lid. When done, brownie will be firm to the touch and a toothpick inserted into the center will come out clean. Serve warm.

PER SERVING:

CALORIES: 327 | **FAT:** 17g | **SODIUM:** 66mg | **CARBOHYDRATES:** 42g | **FIBER:** 3g | **SUGAR:** 31g | **PROTEIN:** 4g

Cinnamon Dulce de Leche

This creamy, delicious topping just got upgraded with a little cinnamon. Use this caramel-style topping as a drizzle on cakes, over ice cream, or as a swirl atop your favorite brownies or cheesecake.

Hands-On Time: 5 minutes
Cook Time: 45 minutes

Serves 16

1 (8-ounce) can sweetened condensed milk
¼ teaspoon baking soda
½ teaspoon ground cinnamon
½ teaspoon vanilla extract
1 cup water

1 In a 6" round baking pan, whisk together sweetened condensed milk, baking soda, cinnamon, and vanilla until well combined. Cover pan tightly with aluminum foil.

2 Pour water into an Instant Pot® and place the trivet in the pot, then place pan on trivet. Place the lid on the Instant Pot® and click into place to close. Press the Pressure Cook button and adjust the timer to 45 minutes. When the timer beeps, let the pressure release naturally, about 20 minutes, then quick-release any remaining pressure until float valve drops. Unlock lid.

3 Carefully remove pan and foil. Dulce de leche will look bubbly and lumpy. Whisk until completely smooth. It will be thick like caramel, and dark brown. Store in an airtight container such as a Mason jar and refrigerate for up to 2 weeks for best freshness.

PER SERVING:

CALORIES: 46 | **FAT:** 1g | **SODIUM:** 37mg | **CARBOHYDRATES:** 8g | **FIBER:** 0g | **SUGAR:** 8g | **PROTEIN:** 1g

Rice Pudding

This warm and comforting old-fashioned dessert is easier to make than ever before in the Instant Pot®. From its perfectly tender rice to its classic creamy texture, this simple pudding is excellent by itself, and is made even better with toppings like chopped strawberries, pecans, or raisins.

Hands-On Time: 10 minutes
Cook Time: 10 minutes

Serves 6

- 1 cup long-grain white rice, rinsed and drained
- 2 cups whole milk
- 1 cup water
- ¼ cup light brown sugar, packed
- 1 teaspoon ground cinnamon
- ¼ teaspoon salt
- ½ teaspoon ground nutmeg
- 1 cup sweetened condensed milk

1 Place rice, whole milk, water, brown sugar, cinnamon, salt, and nutmeg in an Instant Pot® and stir well to combine. Place the lid on the Instant Pot® and click into place to close.

2 Press the Pressure Cook button and adjust the timer to 10 minutes. When the timer beeps, let the pressure release naturally for 10 minutes, then quick-release any remaining pressure until float valve drops. Unlock lid.

3 Stir in sweetened condensed milk until well combined. Press the Cancel button to turn the heat completely off and allow rice pudding to cool 15 minutes, stirring occasionally. It will thicken as it cools. Serve warm.

PER SERVING:

CALORIES: 362 | **FAT:** 7g | **SODIUM:** 200mg | **CARBOHYDRATES:** 66g | **FIBER:** 1g | **SUGAR:** 41g | **PROTEIN:** 9g

Apple Butter

This Apple Butter is simple to make but strong in flavor. The blend of Gala and Granny Smith apples makes this spreadable treat nice and sweet with the perfect tartness. Enjoy on toast or in your oatmeal.

Hands-On Time: 5 minutes
Cook Time: 40 minutes

Serves 24

4 pounds Fuji apples, peeled, cored, and quartered
1½ cups light brown sugar, packed
¼ cup granulated sugar
1 tablespoon ground cinnamon
2 teaspoons apple pie spice
¼ cup pure maple syrup
1 cup water

1 Place all ingredients in an Instant Pot® and stir to combine. Place the lid on the Instant Pot® and click into place to close. Press the Pressure Cook button and adjust the timer to 25 minutes.

2 When the timer beeps, let the pressure release naturally for 15 minutes, then quick-release any remaining pressure until float valve drops. Unlock lid.

3 Use an immersion blender to blend mixture until it is thick and smooth, about 3 minutes. Press the Sauté button on the Instant Pot® and allow mixture to reduce and thicken 15 minutes until desired thickness is reached. Store refrigerated in an airtight container for up to 5 days.

PER SERVING:

CALORIES: 89 | FAT: 0g | SODIUM: 4mg | CARBOHYDRATES: 23g | FIBER: 1g | SUGAR: 21g | PROTEIN: 0g

US/Metric Conversion Chart

VOLUME CONVERSIONS

US Volume Measure	Metric Equivalent
⅛ teaspoon	0.5 milliliter
¼ teaspoon	1 milliliter
½ teaspoon	2 milliliters
1 teaspoon	5 milliliters
½ tablespoon	7 milliliters
1 tablespoon (3 teaspoons)	15 milliliters
2 tablespoons (1 fluid ounce)	30 milliliters
¼ cup (4 tablespoons)	60 milliliters
⅓ cup	90 milliliters
½ cup (4 fluid ounces)	125 milliliters
⅔ cup	160 milliliters
¾ cup (6 fluid ounces)	180 milliliters
1 cup (16 tablespoons)	250 milliliters
1 pint (2 cups)	500 milliliters
1 quart (4 cups)	1 liter (about)

WEIGHT CONVERSIONS

US Weight Measure	Metric Equivalent
½ ounce	15 grams
1 ounce	30 grams
2 ounces	60 grams
3 ounces	85 grams
¼ pound (4 ounces)	115 grams
½ pound (8 ounces)	225 grams
¾ pound (12 ounces)	340 grams
1 pound (16 ounces)	454 grams

OVEN TEMPERATURE CONVERSIONS

Degrees Fahrenheit	Degrees Celsius
200 degrees F	95 degrees C
250 degrees F	120 degrees C
275 degrees F	135 degrees C
300 degrees F	150 degrees C
325 degrees F	160 degrees C
350 degrees F	180 degrees C
375 degrees F	190 degrees C
400 degrees F	205 degrees C
425 degrees F	220 degrees C
450 degrees F	230 degrees C

BAKING PAN SIZES

American	Metric
8 x 1½ inch round baking pan	20 x 4 cm cake tin
9 x 1½ inch round baking pan	23 x 3.5 cm cake tin
11 x 7 x 1½ inch baking pan	28 x 18 x 4 cm baking tin
13 x 9 x 2 inch baking pan	30 x 20 x 5 cm baking tin
2 quart rectangular baking dish	30 x 20 x 3 cm baking tin
15 x 10 x 2 inch baking pan	30 x 25 x 2 cm baking tin (Swiss roll tin)
9 inch pie plate	22 x 4 or 23 x 4 cm pie plate
7 or 8 inch springform pan	18 or 20 cm springform or loose bottom cake tin
9 x 5 x 3 inch loaf pan	23 x 13 x 7 cm or 2 lb narrow loaf or pate tin
1½ quart casserole	1.5 liter casserole
2 quart casserole	2 liter casserole

Index

Note: Page numbers in **bold** indicate recipe category overviews and lists.

Accessory removal options, 9
Appetizers and snacks, **71**–89, 179
Apples
  Apple Butter, 216
  Apple Cinnamon Oatmeal, 12
  Applesauce, 80
  Caramel Apple Cider, 202
  Cinnamon Apple Upside-Down Cake, 201
  Protein-Packed Baked Apples, 199
  Stewed Apples, 198
Artichokes, in Spinach Artichoke Dip, 77
Avocado Lime Chicken Salad, 129

Bacon
  Bacon and Cream Cheese–Stuffed Mushrooms, 85
  Bacon and Onion Quiche, 19
  other recipes with, 37, 45, 47, 61, 66
Banana Bread, 205

Beans and lentils
  about: sorting before rinsing, 59
  Baked Beans, 61
  Barbecue Lentil Sandwiches, 190
  Bean and Rice Burritos, 191
  Black Bean Burgers, 185
  Black Beans, 60
  Chickpea Curry, 178
  Chickpeas, 64
  Chili Cheese Dip, 73
  other soup/chili recipes with, 39, 40–41, 42
  Pinto Beans, 59
  Three-Bean Chili, 175
  Tomato Lentil Soup, 49
Beef. *See also* Meatballs
  Beef Stew, 38
  Cabbage Roll Soup, 43
  Cheeseburger Macaroni, 70
  Cheeseburger Soup, 37
  Chili Cheese Dip, 73
  Lasagna Soup, 31
  Red Chili, 39
  Slow Cooker Beefy Queso Dip, 74
Beef main dishes
  Barbecue Short Ribs, 137
  Beef Stroganoff, 147

Bolognese Sauce, 154
Corned Beef Brisket Sandwiches, 135
Easy Cheeseburgers, 134
Italian-Style Meatballs in Marinara Sauce, 152
Meatloaf, 144–45
Mississippi Pot Roast, 146
Philly Cheesesteak Sandwiches, 151
Sloppy Joes, 149
Slow Cooker Beef and Broccoli, 140
Swedish Meatballs, 153
Taco-Stuffed Peppers, 148
Berries
  Blueberry Pecan Oatmeal, 13
  Cranberry Sauce, 108
  Strawberry Jam, 209
Bread
  about: hamburger bun croutons, 37
  Banana Bread, 205
  Bread Pudding, 204
  Corn Bread, 98
  French Toast Casserole, 28
  Three-Cheese Breakfast Strata, 22
Breakfast, **11**–28
Breakfast Casserole, 27

Broccoli
    Broccoli Cheddar
        Soup, 36
    Chicken Broccoli Al-
        fredo, 118–19
    Slow Cooker Beef and
        Broccoli, 140
    Steamed Lemon Broc-
        coli, 102
Brownies, fudge, 213
Brussels sprouts, lemon
    pepper, 101
Burritos, 21, 191

Cabbage
    Buttery Cabbage, 108
    Cabbage Roll Soup, 43
    Vegetable Dumplings,
        179
Caramel Apple Cider, 202
Caramel Flan, 208
Carrots, maple-glazed,
    104
Cereal, in Ranch Slow
    Cooker Snack Mix, 75
Cheese
    Bacon and Cream
        Cheese–Stuffed
        Mushrooms, 85
    Broccoli Cheddar
        Soup, 36
    Cheeseburger Soup,
        37
    Cheesy Chicken and
        Rice, 128
    Cheesy Smoked Sau-
        sage and Rice, 139
    Chili Cheese Dip, 73
    Crustless Vanilla
        Cheesecake, 196
    Kale and Goat Cheese–
        Stuffed Portobellos,
        186

pasta with. See Pasta
    sandwiches with. See
        Sandwiches and
        wraps
    Slow Cooker Beefy
        Queso Dip, 74
    Three-Cheese Break-
        fast Strata, 22
Chicken
    about: ground chicken
        breast, 82
    Barbecue Wings, 86
    Buffalo Chicken Dip, 73
    Buffalo Chicken Wings,
        89
    Chicken Noodle Soup,
        35
    Creamy Chipotle
        Chicken Soup, 48
    Green Enchilada
        Chicken Soup, 44
    Quick Chicken
        Steamed Rice, 56–57
    Spicy Chicken Sliders,
        82–83
    Taco Soup, 40–41
    White Chicken Chili, 42
    Wild Rice and Chicken
        Soup, 33
Chicken main dishes,
    109–32
    about: making chicken
        gravy, 110
    Avocado Lime Chicken
        Salad, 129
    Barbecue Chicken
        Drumsticks, 121
    Butter Chicken, 125
    Cheesy Chicken and
        Rice, 128
    Chicken and Mashed
        Potato Bowl, 114
    Chicken Broccoli Al-

fredo, 118–19
    Chicken Fajitas, 113
    Creamy Mushroom
        Smothered Chicken,
        126
    Creamy Ranch Chick-
        en, 115
    Hawaiian Chicken,
        130–31
    Italian Chicken Pasta,
        132
    Italian Herb Chicken
        Drumsticks, 120
    Jerk Chicken Thighs,
        116
    Lemon Garlic Chicken
        Thighs, 117
    Lemon Herb Whole
        Chicken, 110
    Pesto Chicken, 123
    Shredded Chicken, 111
    Spicy Chicken Burgers,
        122
    Teriyaki Chicken, 127
Chocolate
    Chocolate Chip Cookie
        Cake, 206–7
    Fudge Brownies, 213
    Slow Cooker Choco-
        late Peanut Clusters,
        211
    Slow Cooker Hot
        Chocolate, 203
Cleaning Instant Pot®, 9,
    10
Coffee cake, cinnamon,
    25
Corn and cornmeal
    Corn Bread, 98
    Corn on the Cob, 104
    Grits, 12
    Popcorn, 87

Desserts, **193**–216

Drinks
    Caramel Apple Cider, 202
    Slow Cooker Hot Chocolate, 203

Dulce de leche, cinnamon, 214

Dumplings, vegetable, and Pierogis, 179, 180

Eggs
    about: Egg button, 7; room-temperature, 66
    Bacon and Onion Quiche, 19
    Breakfast Burritos, 21
    Caramel Flan, 208
    Egg Bites, 23
    French Toast Casserole, 28
    Hard-Cooked Eggs, 72
    Three-Cheese Breakfast Strata, 22
    Vegetable Frittata, 16–17

Fish and seafood main dishes, **155**–72
    about: deveining or deveined shrimp, 163; using fish scraps, 169; white fish, 167
    Cajun Garlic Butter Cod, 167
    Cajun Shrimp and Sausage Boil, 158–59
    Chipotle Lime Shrimp, 163
    Classic Shrimp, 157
    Crab-Stuffed Peppers, 170–71
    Creamy Tuscan Salmon, 168
    Fish Tacos, 165
    Honey Garlic–Glazed Salmon, 162
    Lemon Dill Salmon, 160
    Lobster Tails, 156
    Mussels, 166
    Seafood Stock, 169
    Snow Crab Legs, 157
    Spicy Chili Lime Salmon, 161
    Tomato Steamed Halibut, 172

Flan, caramel, 208

Garlic Spread, 103

Grape Jelly Meatballs, 79

Green Bean Casserole, 105

Green beans, steamed, 99

Instant Pot®
    accessory removal options, 9
    cleaning, 9, 10
    cooking as quickly as possible, 9–10
    functions of, 6–7
    locking and pressure-release methods, 7–8
    pot-in-pot accessories, 8
    pressure cooking benefits, 5–6

Jerk seasoning, and Jerk Chicken Thighs, 117

Kale, dishes with, 47, 186, 187

Keep Warm/Cancel button, 7

Lentils, 49, 190

Locking and pressure-release methods, 7–8

Meatballs, 65, 79, 84, 152, 153

Mushrooms
    Bacon and Cream Cheese–Stuffed Mushrooms, 85
    Creamy Mushroom Smothered Chicken, 126
    Creamy Portobello Risotto, 181
    Kale and Goat Cheese–Stuffed Portobellos, 186
    Mushroom Wild Rice, 54
    Vegetable Dumplings, 179

Nuts
    Blueberry Pecan Oatmeal, 13
    Cajun Boiled Peanuts, 78
    Slow Cooker Candied Pecans, 210
    Slow Cooker Chocolate Peanut Clusters, 211

Oats
    Apple Cinnamon Oatmeal, 12
    Blueberry Pecan Oatmeal, 13
    Steel-Cut Oats, 13

Onions, in Bacon and Onion Quiche, 19

Pancake Bites, 18
Pasta. *See also* Soups, stews, and chilis
about: frozen meatballs and, 65
Buttery Egg Noodles, 67
Carbonara, 66
Cheeseburger Macaroni, 70
Chicken Broccoli Alfredo, 118–19
Creamy Alfredo Penne, 60
Creamy Lemon Orzo, 64
Italian Chicken Pasta, 132
Macaroni and Cheese, 94–95
Pesto Feta Pasta, 63
Quick and Easy Penne, 67
Ravioli Lasagna, 184
Spaghetti, 65
Spinach and Cheese Manicotti, 68–69
Vegetable Lo Mein, 189
Peppers
Crab-Stuffed Peppers, 170–71
Taco-Stuffed Peppers, 148
Pork. *See also* Bacon; Sausage
Barbecue Pulled Pork, 142
Breakfast Burritos, 21
Ginger Orange–Glazed Pork, 143

Hawaiian Pulled Pork Sandwiches, 140
Lime Pulled Pork, 141
Sweet and Spicy Ribs, 136
Potatoes
Baked Potatoes, 92
Breakfast Potatoes, 15
Chicken and Mashed Potato Bowl, 114
Mashed Potatoes, 96
Mustard Potato Salad, 97
Petite Golden Potatoes, 93
Pierogis, 180
Steakhouse Potato Chowder, 45
Tuscan Soup, 47
Pressure Cook button, 6
Pressure-release methods, 7–8
Pudding, bread, 204
Pudding Cake, 194–95

Quinoa and Sweet Potato Bowl, 187

Rice and wild rice
Bean and Rice Burritos, 191
Cajun-Style Rice, 55
Cheesy Chicken and Rice, 128
Cheesy Smoked Sausage and Rice, 139
Cilantro Lime Rice, 53
Creamy Portobello Risotto, 181
Long-Grain White Rice, 54
Mexican-Style Rice, 58

Mushroom Wild Rice, 54
Quick Chicken Steamed Rice, 56–57
Rice Pudding, 215
Risotto, 52
Wild Rice and Chicken Soup, 33

Sandwiches and wraps
Barbecue Lentil Sandwiches, 190
Bean and Rice Burritos, 191
Black Bean Burgers, 185
Breakfast Burritos, 21
Chicken Fajitas, 113
Corned Beef Brisket Sandwiches, 135
Easy Cheeseburgers, 134
Fish Tacos, 165
Hawaiian Pulled Pork Sandwiches, 140
Sloppy Joes, 149
Spicy Chicken Burgers, 122
Spicy Chicken Sliders, 82–83
Sauces
Bolognese Sauce, 154
Chicken Gravy, 110
Chili Garlic Sauce, 161
Chipotle Sauce, 165
Cranberry Sauce, 108
Garlic Spread, 103
Restaurant-Style Red Salsa, 81
Sausage Gravy, 24
Sausage
Barbecue Mini Smoked Sausages, 80

Breakfast Sausage Links, 24

Cajun Shrimp and Sausage Boil, 158–59

Cheesy Smoked Sausage and Rice, 139

Creamy Sausage and Tortellini Soup, 30

other recipes with, 47, 154

Sausage Gravy, 24

Sauté button, 7

Seafood. *See* Fish and seafood main dishes

Side dishes, **91**–108

Slow Cook button, 6

Snacks and appetizers, **71**–89, 179

Soups, stews, and chilis, **29**–49, 175, 177

Soups, stews, and chilis, Instant Pot® buttons for, 6, 7

Spinach and Cheese Manicotti, 68–69

Spinach Artichoke Dip, 77

Squash

Butternut Squash Chili, 177

Cinnamon Butternut Squash, 106–7

Italian Zucchini, 182–83

Spaghetti Squash, 174

Steam button, 6

Strawberry Jam, 209

Sweet potatoes, 187, 192

Tomatoes. *See also* Sauces

Tomato Lentil Soup, 49

Tomato Soup, 32

Tomato Steamed Halibut, 172

Turkey meatballs, mini Greek, 84

Vanilla cheesecake, crustless, 196

Vanilla Pound Cake, 197

Vegetables. *See also specific vegetables*

Vegetable Frittata, 16–17

Vegetable Lo Mein, 189

Vegetarian main dishes, **173**–92

Yogurt, 14

Yogurt button, 7

Zucchini, Italian, 182–83